# Marketer's
# Toolkit

## Harvard Business Essentials

*The New Manager's Guide and Mentor*

The Harvard Business Essentials series is designed to provide comprehensive advice, personal coaching, background information, and guidance on the most relevant topics in business. Drawing on rich content from Harvard Business School Publishing and other sources, these concise guides are carefully crafted to provide a highly practical resource for readers with all levels of experience, and will prove especially valuable for the new manager. To assure quality and accuracy, each volume is closely reviewed by a specialized content adviser from a world-class business school. Whether you are a new manager seeking to expand your skills or a seasoned professional looking to broaden your knowledge base, these solution-oriented books put reliable answers at your fingertips.

Other books in the series:

*Finance for Managers*
*Hiring and Keeping the Best People*
*Managing Change and Transition*
*Negotiation*
*Business Communication*
*Managing Projects Large and Small*
*Manager's Toolkit*
*Crisis Management*
*Entrepreneur's Toolkit*
*Time Management*
*Power, Influence, and Persuasion*
*Strategy*
*Decision Making*

HARVARD
BUSINESS
ESSENTIALS

# Marketer's Toolkit

*The 10 Strategies You
Need to Succeed*

Harvard Business School Press | *Boston, Massachusetts*

No part of this publication may be reproduced, stored in or introduced into a retrieval system, or transmitted, in any form, or by any means (electronic, mechanical, photo-copying, recording, or otherwise), without the prior permission of the publisher. Requests for permission should be directed to permissions@hbsp.harvard.edu, or mailed to Permissions, Harvard Business School Publishing, 60 Harvard Way, Boston, Massachusetts 02163.

978-1-59139-762-5 (ISBN 13)

**Library of Congress Cataloging-in-Publication Data**

Harvard business essentials : marketer's toolkit : the 10 strategies you need to succeed.

p. cm. — (Harvard business essentials series)

Includes bibliographical references and index.

ISBN 1-59139-762-6

1. Marketing—Handbooks, manuals, etc. 2. Strategic planning—Handbooks, manuals, etc. I. Harvard Business School. II. Series.

HF5415.H24333 2006

658.8'02—dc22

2005020520

# Contents

**Introduction**                                                    **xi**

**1  Marketing Strategy**                                            **1**
*How It Fits with Business Strategy*

What Is Strategy?                                                     2
The Strategy Process                                                 4
Where Marketing Fits In                                              5
Marketing Strategy and Product Life Cycles                           8
Summing Up                                                          16

**2  Creating a Marketing Plan**                                     **19**
*An Overview*

From Strategy to Plan                                               20
Implementing Your Plan via the Marketing Mix                        21
Controlling Plan Implementation                                     28
Summing Up                                                          29

**3  Market Research**                                               **31**
*Listen and Learn*

Formal Market Research                                              33
Two Formal Methods for Analyzing
    Buyer Preferences                                               35
Informal Research Methods: Close Customer Contact                   43
Summing Up                                                          50

**4   Market Customization**                                    **51**
*Segmentation, Targeting, and Positioning*

   Segmentation                                             54
   From Segmentation to Targeting                           58
   Positioning                                              60
   Summing Up                                               63

**5   Competitor Analysis**                                     **65**
*Understand Your Opponents*

   Who Are Your Competitors?                                67
   Characteristics for Analysis                             69
   Porter's Five Forces Framework                           73
   Summing Up                                               75

**6   Branding**                                                **77**
*Differentiation That Customers Value*

   Differentiation of Commodity
     Products and Services                               79
   Approaches to Differentiation                            81
   Differentiation That Matters                             86
   Summing Up                                               87

**7   The Right Customers**                                     **89**
*Acquisition, Retention, and Development*

   Customer Economics                                       90
   Customer Retention                                       96
   Customer Development                                     99
   Summing Up                                              102

**8   Developing New Products and Services**                   **103**
*The Marketer's Role*

   The Two Types of New Products                           105
   Extending Product Lines into New Segments               109
   The New-Product Process                                 112
   The Marketer's Role                                     117
   Your New-Product Strategy                               120

Beyond New                                              120

Summing Up                                              122

**9   Pricing It Right                                  125**
*Strategies, Applications, and Pitfalls*

Cost-Plus Pricing                                       127

Price Skimming                                          128

Penetration Pricing                                     130

Exploiting the Experience Curve                         132

Prestige Pricing                                        133

Bait and Hook Pricing                                   134

Price Promotions                                        135

Customer-Perceived Value: The Ultimate Arbiter of Price  138

Pricing and the Product Life Cycle                      139

Summing Up                                              142

**10  Integrated Marketing Communications              145**
*Creativity, Consistency, and Effective Resource Allocation*

The Goal of Marketing Communications                    147

Communication Vehicles                                  148

Putting It All Together                                 152

The Management Challenge                                153

Summing Up                                              154

**11  Interactive Marketing                            157**
*New Channel, New Challenge*

Growing Online Sales                                    158

E-mail Marketing                                        162

Web-Based Merchandising                                 166

Summing Up                                              169

**12  Marketing Across Borders                         171**
*It's a Big, Big World*

Product Decisions                                       173

Promotion                                               177

Place (or Distribution)                                 178

Price                                                     179

Controlling Global Marketing Decisions                    180

Summing Up                                                182

13   **The Future of Marketing**                          **185**
     *Tomorrow's Challenges*

     Today's Buyers Have More Information                 186

     Delivering on the Promise                            187

     Cutting Through the Clutter                          188

     Market Fragmentation                                 190

     Measurement and Accountability                       191

     The Ethics of Marketing                              193

     Summing Up                                           195

     **Appendix: Useful Implementation Tools**            **197**

     **Notes**                                            **203**

     **Glossary**                                         **207**

     **For Further Reading**                              **215**

     **Index**                                            **223**

     **About the Subject Adviser**                        **229**

     **About the Writer**                                 **230**

# Marketer's
# Toolkit

# Introduction

This book is about marketing, covering its foundation concepts as well as its more challenging contemporary issues, such as online and global marketing. If you are new to this subject—perhaps as an engineer, a salesperson, a product developer, or a technical professional taking on management responsibilities—*Marketer's Toolkit* will familiarize you with concepts you need to understand.

Everyone in every company needs to understand marketing. If you are already involved in marketing—for example, as a researcher, a sales representative, a customer service manager, or an e-commerce site manager—this book will broaden your understanding of the discipline and show you how its many parts can be brought to bear in a coherent and effective marketing strategy and plan.

## The Market Orientation

*Marketing* is both a business function and a business orientation. Most of us think only of its functions—the things that marketing people do: sales, promotion, advertising, market research, distribution, public relations, and so forth. Indeed, most of the money spent on marketing is directed to these activities and the personnel who handle them.

Until the early 1950s, the marketing function effectively owned the customers of the business—"owned" in the sense that marketing had sole responsibility for customers and provided the communication link between customers and the company. Everyone else in the company was responsible for making products and getting them to the loading dock; marketing's job was to sell them. This arrangement stemmed from what has become known as the *production orientation* (see figure I-1). This orientation is based on the belief that people will buy products that are inexpensive and readily available. It is the mind-set of mass production and the early Industrial Age: make things and push them out to the market.

This product push orientation worked very well during the nineteenth and early twentieth centuries, an era in which basic human material wants were high relative to production and competition. It was an era in which the market could absorb, for example, as many inexpensive Model T automobiles as Henry Ford could run off his new-fangled assembly line, and as many ten-dollar Kodak cameras and rolls of film as George Eastman could turn out. These and hundreds of other products were new, and they were welcomed by a buying public that owned few material things.

The production orientation led people to believe that the marketing staff—salespeople, ad writers, order fulfillment personnel, and so forth—had sole responsibility for customers. Everyone else

**FIGURE I-1**

**The production orientation**

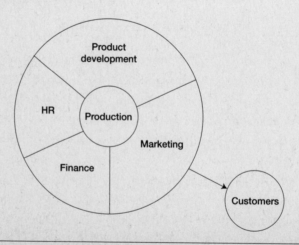

could hunker down inside the walls of the company, concentrate on other work, and never talk to, study, or even think about the people who bought their products and services.

Although the production orientation is still alive and well in undeveloped economies, it lost its power elsewhere as once-untapped markets became saturated, as competition grew, and as buyers began looking for greater value and uniqueness in the things they bought. This led to an important shift to an orientation in which a knowledge of customer needs gained in importance. Thus, Alfred Sloan would tell General Motors stockholders in 1933 that GM's consumer research department had invited one million North American motorists "to pool their practical experience with the technical skills of General Motors engineers and designers." This was unprecedented. Sloan went an important step further in this same letter:

> To discuss consumer research as a functional activity would give an erroneous impression. In its broad implications it is more in the nature of an OPERATING PHILOSOPHY, which, to be fully effective, must extend through all phases of a business—weighing every action from the standpoint of how it affects the goodwill of the institution, recognizing that the quickest way to profits—and the permanent assurance of such profits—is to serve the customer in ways in which the customer wants to be served.[1]

What Sloan was articulating, perhaps for the first time in print, has become known as the *market orientation*. The market orientation holds that a company must understand what customers want, need, and value and then must organize itself to produce and deliver the products and services customers truly value. Decades later, business philosopher Peter Drucker picked up Sloan's idea with a now famous quotation: "There is only one valid definition of business purpose: to create a customer."[2]

The market orientation shifted the focus of business management from the wheels of production to the understanding and service of customers (figure I-2). Its implications for managers and employees are profound. Marketing no longer owns the customer; customers must be everyone's primary concern. As David Packard

**FIGURE I-2**

## The market orientation

once put it, "Marketing is too important to be left solely to the marketing department." Whether your job is handling finance, designing new products, training new employees, or scheduling production runs, you must be conscious of how your work affects customers, because, in the end, customer satisfaction is the foremost ingredient in long-term profitability. Vincent Barabba articulated this new orientation when he wrote, "If you provide customers with innovative solutions to what they want and need, keep your costs below what your customers are willing to pay, and make sure your employees are healthy, motivated, and informed, all else should follow—profits, growth, a sense of accomplishment and service, and favorable recognition by the communities with which you exist."[3]

What is your company's *market orientation*? Are its various functions oriented toward customers, or is responsibility for customers left entirely in the hands of marketing? Hopefully, it's the former. In either case, the material in this book can help you understand how you can connect with customers through strategy, action plans, research, and other activities. Being an "essentials" book, it cannot make you an expert, but it will make you knowledgeable in key areas and get you going in the right direction.

# What's Ahead

Here's a preview of how the material is presented. We begin with strategy, which describes how you differentiate yourself from your competitors and apply your resources. Business strategy drives all the key activities of an organization, including marketing.

Chapter 1 provides a primer on business strategy and explains how marketing is aligned with it. It also describes the product life cycle: introduction, growth, maturity, and decline. A company needs a marketing strategy for products and services in each of these phases, and knowing about the product life cycle helps you think about what your marketing strategy should be and when you should change it. This discussion leads naturally into the topic of chapter 2: the marketing plan, which lays out a campaign that translates the strategy into specific actions. The plan states exactly what the company will do on the marketing front, who will do it, and when.

Successful businesses remain so by constantly scanning the external environment for new opportunities—a process of listening and learning. Chapter 3 describes formal and informal methods for doing this, and it presents two useful research tools—concept testing and conjoint analysis—for analyzing customer preferences.

Chapter 4 covers three of the most useful techniques in the marketer's toolkit: segmentation, targeting, and positioning. Some products and services, such as electricity and concrete, have universal appeal, but most do not. Most products and services must be developed with the particular needs and preferences of various market segments in mind. This chapter describes the purpose of segmentation and looks at the basics of segmenting a market in terms of multiple factors. It goes on to show how you can then target the segments that have the greatest business potential, and position your offering to make it stand out.

After you've identified an attractive segment, you must size up the competitive situation it represents. Understanding your opponents is sometimes half the battle. Chapter 5 can help you size up that situation by determining who your competitors are. What are their strategies and objectives? What are their strengths and weaknesses relative to your own? And how aggressively will these competitors respond to your moves?

Chapters 1 through 5 cover fundamental concepts that everyone in marketing must regularly understand and apply. They are the hammers and wrenches in the marketer's toolkit. The remaining chapters address cutting-edge issues that many marketers and their colleagues are wrestling with. Branding is the first of these. By some reports, there are now more than two million brands in the market, and another four hundred to seven hundred appear daily. The point of developing a brand image is to make a product or service stand out, but how can that happen in so crowded a universe? Chapter 6 considers the important business of making your offering stand out from the pack. It reviews various approaches to differentiation and even shows how commodity products can take on the aura of a distinctive brand.

Many companies work hard at developing a continuing relationship with customers. This is particularly true for financial services companies (banking, credit cards, insurance), consultancies, supplier companies, hotel chains, and even grocery stores. These businesses depend on repeat customers and aim to gain a larger "share of the wallet" from them over time. Chapter 7 probes the building blocks of relationship marketing: customer acquisition, retention, and development. It presents economics concepts you can use to differentiate profitable from unprofitable customers. Once you've done that, you'll know how to position your offering and focus your marketing resources to do the most good.

Chapter 8 is about the marketer's role in developing new products. As product (and service) offerings mature and their sales gradually decline, you must either reinvigorate them or replace them with new ones. It's a tricky business. Much money and energy is expended on product development, but only the fittest survive the journey from idea to opportunity recognition to commercialization. This chapter will familiarize you with the development process and the many contributions that marketers can make to it.

Pricing—one of the four elements of the marketing mix—is the subject of chapter 9, which explains price strategies along with their advantages and disadvantages. These include cost-plus pricing; price skimming; penetration pricing; prestige pricing; bait and hook pricing; price promotions; and pricing based on customer-perceived value. We'll also revisit the product life cycle in terms of pricing decisions.

Marketers use various forms of communication to make people aware of their products and services and to move potential customers along to the point of making a purchase. These forms of communication include advertising, personal selling, direct mail, and so forth. With many modes of communication available, marketing managers must find a way to produce a consistent brand message at each customer touch point. Chapter 10 describes a process for doing this. It's called integrated marketing communications (IMC).

Internet marketing, the topic of chapter 11, is a huge deal, accounting for $110 billion to $170 billion in annual U.S. sales alone. The Internet is growing fast, and it has lots of potential for attracting, retaining, and developing customers in an efficient, cost-effective way. Are you taking advantage of this remarkable distribution channel? If you are looking for ideas, this chapter offers practical tips on e-mail campaigns and Web-based marketing.

Chapter 12, on global marketing, examines the key issues that face marketers as they look for customers beyond their own borders. Some of these are fundamentally the same as those you face in evaluating domestic market segments: is the market attractive? Can you sell the same products to this market, or must you customize your offering to satisfy this segment's specific preferences? How can you create awareness and establish brand recognition? This chapter addresses these questions in the cross-border context.

Our final chapter, 13, looks at some of the issues that will challenge marketers in the years ahead.

Like every business function, marketing uses a number of unique terms: *brand equity,* the *marketing mix,* and *vertical product line,* to name a few. We have italicized these important terms in the text. That's your cue that the definition, and sometimes an example, can be found in the Glossary at the end of the book.

We've also provided an appendix of useful tools that were first developed for our online publication, Harvard ManageMentor®. One is a template you can use as you develop your marketing plan. The second appendix tool—"Calculating the value of a customer"—can help you think through what your customers value, using an equation format. The third tool will help you estimate the lifetime value of individual customers. An interactive, Excel-based version of this worksheet can be freely accessed and downloaded from the Harvard Business Essentials Series Web site at www.elearning.hbsp.org/businesstools. While you're at that site, check out the online tools associated with other books in the series; you may find several of them useful in non-marketing aspects of your work.

Because this is an "essentials" book, we had to be selective about what we included in this volume. There is a lot more to marketing than what we've covered here. If you want to learn more, you should refer to "For Further Reading," also located at the end of the book. There you'll find a great many useful Web sites, articles, and books that can add greatly to your learning.

# 1

# Marketing Strategy

*How It Fits with Business Strategy*

## Key Topics Covered in This Chapter

- *The basics of business strategy*

- *Aligning marketing strategy with business strategy*

- *How market strategy changes in the phases of the product or service life cycle*

**W**HAT IS YOUR company's marketing strategy? Do you have a strategy for pricing and distribution? Do you plan to tap customers in Latin America? Are you scheduling a rollout of print and TV ads for a soon-to-be-released new product?

These are important questions because every business needs a marketing strategy. We cannot really talk about marketing strategy, however, without first discussing business strategy. That's because everything you do in marketing must be aligned with your business strategy.

This chapter explains the basics of your business and marketing strategies and shows how you can get them to work together. It also describes the product life cycle phases of introduction, growth, maturity, and decline and explains how marketing strategy must change with each phase.

## What Is Strategy?

In its original sense, *strategy* (from the Greek word *strategos*) is a military term used to describe the art of the general. It refers to the general's plan for arraying and maneuvering his forces with the goal of defeating an enemy army. Carl von Clausewitz, a nineteenth-century theoretician of the art of war, described strategy as "drafting the plan of war and shaping the individual campaigns, and within these, deciding on the individual engagements."[1] More recently, historian Edward Mead Earle has described it as "the art of controlling and utilizing the resources of a nation—or a coalition of nations—including its armed forces, to the end that its vital interests shall be effectively promoted and secured."[2]

Businesspeople have always liked military analogies, so it is not surprising that they have embraced this notion of strategy. They too think of strategy as a plan for controlling and utilizing their resources (human, physical, and financial capital) to the end of promoting and securing their vital interests. Harvard professor Michael Porter has defined strategy as "a broad formula for how a business is going to compete."[3] Inevitably, the formula for competing involves being different in a way that confers a competitive advantage. "Competitive strategy is about being different," wrote Porter. "It means deliberately choosing a different set of activities to deliver a unique mix of value."[4] Consider these familiar examples:

- Southwest Airlines didn't become the most profitable air carrier in North America by copying its rivals. Instead, it differentiated itself with a strategy of low fares, frequent departures, point-to-point service, and customer-pleasing service.

- eBay created a different way for people to sell and acquire goods: online auctions. Company founders aimed for the online service to serve the same purpose as classified ads, flea markets, and formal auctions, but they made it simple, efficient, and wide reaching. Online auctions have differentiated the company's service from those of traditional competitors.

So far, these strategies have served their initiators well and have provided competitive advantages over rivals. Southwest Airlines is the most profitable U.S. air carrier, and eBay is the most successful Internet company ever. Being different can take many forms. As you'll see, even companies whose products are identical to competitors' can strategically set themselves apart by, for example, offering a better price or providing faster and more reliable delivery.

Being "different," of course, does not in itself confer competitive advantage nor ensure business success. The difference must be something that customers value. A rocket car would be "different" but probably would not attract enough customers to be successful. In contrast, a hybrid car—one powered by gasoline and electricity—is different in a way that creates superior value for customers in terms of fuel economy and low emissions of air-fouling exhaust. Those are values for which many people will gladly open their wallets.

So, what is strategy? *Strategy* is a plan that aims to give the enterprise a competitive advantage over rivals. Strategy is about understanding what you do, knowing what you want to become, and—most important—focusing on how you plan to get there. A sound strategy, skillfully implemented, identifies the goals and direction that managers and employees at every level use to define their work and make their organization successful. An organization without a clear strategy, in contrast, is rudderless. It flails about, dashing off in one direction and then another as opportunities present themselves, but achieving very little.

## The Strategy Process

As with most important things in business, you should approach the creation and implementation of strategy as a process—that is, as a set of activities that transforms inputs into outputs. This process is shown in figure 1-1. Here you see that you create strategy based on the company's mission statement, which defines its purpose and articulates what it aims to do for customers and other stakeholders.

Given the mission, senior management sets goals. These goals are tangible manifestations of the organization's mission and are used for planning activities and measuring progress. Goals, as shown in the figure, should be informed by a pragmatic understanding of two things: the external business and market environment, and the internal capabilities of the organization.

Typically, you begin creating a strategy by performing extensive research and analysis and conducting a process through which senior

**FIGURE 1-1**

**The strategy process**

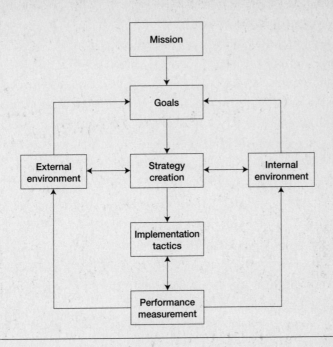

management identifies the top-priority issues that the company needs to tackle to be successful in the long term. For each priority issue, units and teams create high-level action plans. Once you have developed these action plans, you further clarify the company's high-level strategic objectives and direction.

By undertaking the planning process together, senior management and unit leaders ensure that a company's strategies—corporate and unit—are tightly aligned and that successful implementation can follow.

## Where Marketing Fits In

Every activity within the enterprise must align itself with the business strategy. It must do its part to achieve top-level goals and, ultimately, the company's stated mission. In well-managed companies, every employee from the executive suite to the mailroom can state the company's mission and goals and describe how his or her daily tasks contribute to achieving them.

Every function must likewise align its goals and activities with the larger business strategy. In the case of marketing, this means that everything it does—from pricing, to distribution, to how it communicates with customers—should be planned in a way that serves strategic goals. So important is marketing, in fact, that it should help guide the creation of business strategy. If competitive advantage is about "being different," management must answer this two-part question: *what* difference is valued, and *by whom*?

Management naturally turns to marketing for the answers. As the primary link between the enterprise and the external world of competitors and potential customers—through market research and continual customer contact—marketing is often in the best possible position to know what customers need and value. And that knowledge goes to the heart of business strategy at both the corporate and the operating-unit levels. Business strategists look to marketing practitioners primarily for input on the following:

- Competitive threats

- Profitable opportunities

- Areas of market growth, maturity, and decline

- Latent and explicit customer needs

- Ideas for distribution and pricing

In providing this information, marketers not only participate in strategic planning but also develop plans and tactics at various levels: corporate, business unit, and product line. For example, we've noted that Southwest Airlines' strategy is to differentiate itself through low fares, frequent departures, point-to-point service, and customer-pleasing service. Its marketers must develop plans around that strategy. At the corporate level, it must communicate the Southwest message to travelers in general: "We'll get you where you want to go, when you want to go, and at a price you'll like. And you'll enjoy the trip." At the route level, marketing people must think more tactically; they must determine optimal pricing for tickets on each route, the departure times most likely to please travelers, and the advertising messages that will encourage people to make Southwest their first choice on a particular route. The marketers must also examine the business potential of new routes: what is the demand for travel between city A and city B? Which air carrier is currently serving this route? Would customers entertain another option? Thus, marketing people engage in many activities, all aimed at serving the company's strategic goals.

At its heart, a marketing strategy answers the question, Why should our customers buy *our* product (or service) and not those of our competitors? This strategy will later form the heart of the marketing plan for the company's offering.

Marketing strategy, like business strategy, happens on several levels within an organization (figure 1-2). In big companies, people create strategy at the corporate level, at the level of the strategic business unit (SBU), and at the product-line level. In many smaller companies, strategy may be created on all three levels simultaneously. In fact, a product manager developing a market strategy at a small firm might ask, "How should we market this product?" Answering that strategic question requires a clear understanding of the product's competitive advantage—or, from the customer's perspective, the need that the product fulfills more effectively than rival products.

The marketing strategy also defines the following:

- **The target market.** An example might be educated and affluent drivers.

- **How the product or service will be positioned to appeal to that market.** For example, "Our consulting service brings together deep industry knowledge with state-of-the art problem solutions."

- **How the product will be branded.** A product *brand* is a name, term, sign, symbol, or design—or any combination of these— that identifies the offering and differentiates it from those of competitors. For example, "Coca Cola" identifies a unique cola-based soft drink.

**FIGURE 1-2**

## Marketing and business strategy

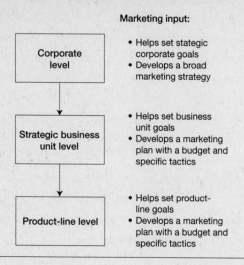

Marketing input:

| | |
|---|---|
| **Corporate level** | • Helps set stategic corporate goals<br>• Develops a broad marketing strategy |
| **Strategic business unit level** | • Helps set business unit goals<br>• Develops a marketing plan with a budget and specific tactics |
| **Product-line level** | • Helps set product-line goals<br>• Develops a marketing plan with a budget and specific tactics |

Every strategist must understand the external environment. For marketers, this means having a firm grasp on the following:

- The target market's size, demographic characteristics, and typical behavior

- The primary benefit of the proposed product *as seen by customers*

- An estimate of sales, market share, and profits that the product could generate over the next few years

Marketing strategy is general by nature. As you'll see later in this book, the details of strategy implementation are picked up in the marketing plan.

## Marketing Strategy and Product Life Cycles

Marketplace realities for a type of product or service generally change over time. For example, a new product concept—such as a television set, a personal computer, a personal digital assistant (PDA), or a cell phone—goes through four life cycle phases, as shown in figure 1-3: introduction, growth, maturity, and decline. Each phase presents a unique challenge to marketers, who must create a strategy for generating sales that recognizes the circumstances of each phase.

Consider the case of the personal computer. When the first personal computers appeared in the late 1970s, only a small segment of the population showed any interest: technologists, mathematicians, and hobbyists. Many PCs were sold as kits. Apple Computer and other manufacturers introduced improved models that simplified setup and use. Software writers provided programs that made these machines useful for a wide range of tasks. When IBM jumped into the game in 1981, the market grew rapidly. Industrywide sales jumped

**FIGURE 1-3**

**Typical product life cycle**

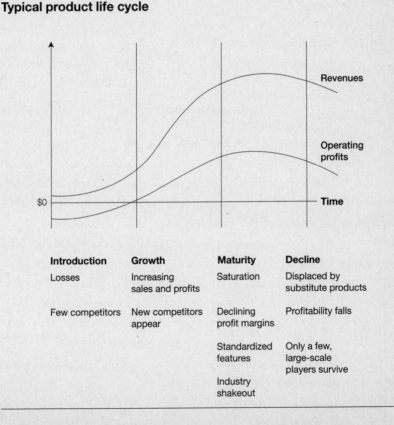

| Introduction | Growth | Maturity | Decline |
|---|---|---|---|
| Losses | Increasing sales and profits | Saturation | Displaced by substitute products |
| Few competitors | New competitors appear | Declining profit margins | Profitability falls |
| | | Standardized features | Only a few, large-scale players survive |
| | | Industry shakeout | |

higher every quarter, and many new competitors, attracted by those rising sales, entered the business. Before long, many people had a desktop machine at work and another at home, and they would replace these every two or three years as new and improved models were developed. PCs were on the sharp, upward growth slope of the life cycle.

By the late 1990s, only twenty years after Apple introduced its landmark Apple II machine, the personal computer industry had taken on many of the characteristics of market maturity: a slower rate of unit sales due to market saturation, price resistance from customers, a declining rate of technical product improvements, and declining profitability. The PC was becoming a commodity product, like the refrigerator and the television set. In this phase only large-scale producers could prosper. Thus, small firms dropped out. Hewlett-Packard purchased rival Compaq in quest of the scale it felt was required to operate profitably. IBM sold its PC operations to a Chinese manufacturer.

Marketing strategy must change in each phase of the life cycle. Let's consider how.

### The Introduction Phase

In this phase, one or more pioneers attempt to draw attention to something new and unfamiliar. Marketing's job is twofold: to create awareness of the product category and educate potential customers in how they can use it to their benefit. Consider again the personal computer. In the late 1970s, Apple, Atari, PET, Radio Shack, and other pioneers were as interested in creating the market as in pushing their particular products. Growing awareness and interest in personal computing was good for all competitors. When giant IBM entered the market in 1981, the existing players were overjoyed because Big Blue's entry gave their product category legitimacy and would bring more people into the market.

Product-line financial losses are typical in this start-up phase as revenues are quickly eaten up by continued product development, marketing, and manufacturing costs.

The marketing challenge in the start-up phase is to create product awareness and get people to try the product. The aim is to make the pie grow bigger.

## The Growth Phase

Some products experience a stage of rapid revenue growth. Net income shoots upward, ending start-up losses. In some cases, however, only a small portion of those revenues makes it to the bottom line (net profits). The reason is that the company (or product line) is busily reinvesting its operating profits in product development, brand building, and market expansion. eBay, the online auction giant, illustrates the point.

eBay began operations in 1995 as a home-based business. The concept of buying and selling through an online auction was so appealing, however, that it grew quickly. Figure 1-4 indicates the magnitude of

**FIGURE 1-4**

**eBay revenues and net income during formative years (1996–2002)**

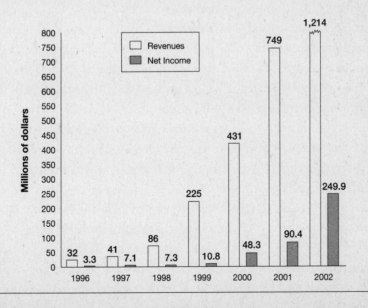

that growth in the company's formative period, 1996–2002. Notice that net income barely inched up during 1997–1999, even though revenue was more than doubling year to year. In the absence of other information, we might think that eBay was doing a poor job of managing its bottom line. In fact, the company was using cash generated through revenues to develop its online infrastructure, create a recognizable brand, and develop new auction categories. It was also aggressively staking claims in other segments of the auction universe, often through acquisition; this preempted market entry by potential rivals.

> The marketing challenge in the growth phase is to switch from creating product awareness to brand building. Because new competitors are naturally drawn to the rising level of revenues and profits, you should concentrate on maximizing the company's shares of the growing pie. To capture more revenues, extend the product; an example is Apple's 2005 introduction of the lower-priced iPod Mini.

### The Maturity Phase

Eventually, most industries and product categories reach a point of maturity, which is characterized by a consolidation in the number of producers, flat or slow unit sales growth, and declining profit margins. In the maturity phase, the seller's market gives way to a buyer's market. Margins decline as producers wrestle with each other in trying to capture a bigger slice of pie. Product changes are incremental, not "breakthrough." Substantial sums are spent on advertising and price discounts. Competition deteriorates into a punching match between entrenched competitors, each trying to win a point or two of market share from the others.

The personal computer industry is very near the maturity phase, if not in it. Hardware and software makers continue to make incremental improvements, but these have not excited consumers and businesses to the point that they will dump their current machines in favor of new ones. Even Microsoft has discovered that big corporate customers are less and less willing to replace their "office suite" software with Microsoft's latest versions. These customers feel that the purchase and training costs associated with those replacements are not justified by new bells and whistles. PC vendors have come up against similar resistance and must resort to price discounts to move their merchandise.

As with other life cycle phases, the transition from rapid growth to maturity requires a strategy shift on the part of marketers, one that recognizes a change in supply and demand. Here, you attempt to differentiate on price and on any new features your R&D people have integrated into the mature product. If you watch the very mature auto industry, you'll see the mature phase marketing strategy in action. In the saturated U.S. market, for example, automakers resort to low-cost or zero-percent financing to move the merchandise. They tout new technical gizmos, such as GM's OnStar GPS and emergency road service feature. They offer new technologies to set themselves apart, such as all-wheel drive on passenger cars.

"New and improved"—you've probably heard it a thousand times to describe mature products. Indeed, strategy in the mature phase tries to revitalize brands in ways that will increase revenues. Figure 1-5 represents the goal of brand revitalization. It indicates the start-up, rapid growth, and maturity phases, as well as the beginnings of decline for a particular brand. The bold line represents what business and marketing strategists attempt through some form of brand revitalization, whose aim is to get the brand back on the growth track. Here are some examples of product revitalization:

- Wireless features added to traditional laptop computers

- GPS applications in passenger cars

- Plaque-fighting ingredients added to traditional toothpaste

- New uses for an old product (for example, Arm & Hammer's campaign to boost sales of baking soda by suggesting that people freshen the air in their refrigerators by putting an open box on the shelf or reduce odors in cat litter boxes by mixing in the product)

**FIGURE 1-5**

**Brand revitalization**

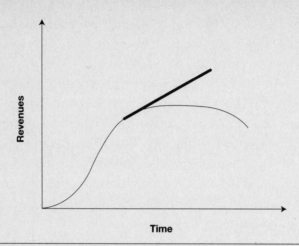

Marketing's role in brand revitalization strategy is twofold:

1. Work with product developers to determine what customers will value and what they will pay for.

2. When the new-and-improved product is launched, communicate with the marketplace about the greater value it now represents.

The great danger in a brand revitalization strategy is getting the first of these assignments wrong. It's easy to be myopic about product "improvements." Managers have a bad habit of thinking that customers should be as excited as they are about whatever new feature the R&D people have cooked up, when in fact customers couldn't care less. Managers think about their differentiating features quite a bit; customers think about these feature hardly at all. Managers spend millions advertising their differentiating features, and customers ignore them.

In the early 1990s, for example, some Japanese car makers were so excited about their flexible manufacturing capabilities that they offered customers the ability to choose between dozens of options for steering wheels, sound system packages, floor carpets, wheel covers, and so on. The variety was mind-boggling—and that was the problem. Customers didn't want their minds boggled! The many choices were not valued—in fact, customers viewed them negatively. What they wanted was a simple set of choices.

> The marketing challenges in the mature phase include the need to protect market share through intensified promotion, to reduce manufacturing costs as price pressure becomes more intense, to eliminate weaknesses in the product, and to leverage the success of the current brands with brand extensions.

## The Decline Phase

Every dog has his day, as folk wisdom puts it. The same can be said of many products and services. In the decline phase, unit sales diminish year after year. One reason is technical obsolescence. For example, sales of vacuum tubes diminished rapidly, beginning in the 1950s, as newly developed transistors displaced them in most types of electronic devices. Vacuum tubes survive today only in a few specialized applications.

Changing buyer behavior is another reason for decline. The manufacturers of men's suits have taken a big hit in recent years as workplace dress codes have become more informal. The sales of sewing machines and fabric also declined as women entered the workforce; these working women lacked the time and energy to make their own clothes, as they had in the past.

> The marketing challenges in the decline phase include the need to promote new uses for old products and introduce the product in new markets—for example, by selling in parts of the developing world. One European food company did that with its baby formula. With birthrates in decline in Europe and North America—its initial stronghold—it began selling baby formula in Africa, where this ordinary product was viewed as a status item. Marketers must aim to harvest as much profit as possible from the brand.

Not every product or service can be defined through this life cycle approach. Life is not that tidy. However, the life cycle is a useful tool for anticipating future challenges and assessing how you can respond.

Take a minute to think about your company's products and services. Which of the life cycle phases do they currently occupy? What are your marketing people doing to improve sales and profit performance?

## Summing Up

- Competitive strategy is about being different in a way that customers value.

- In formulating a strategy, management must determine *what* difference is valued and *by whom*.

- Marketing strategy must be aligned with business strategy. It answers the question, Why should our customers buy *our* product (or service) and not those of our competitors?

- Marketing strategy defines the target market, how the product or service will be positioned, and how it will be branded.

- A new product concept goes through four life cycle phases: introduction, growth, maturity, and decline. Each phase presents a different challenge to marketers.

- In the introduction phase, marketing's job is to create awareness of the product category and to educate potential customers about how they can use it to their benefit.

- Products or services that experience a phase of rapid unit sales growth attract competitors. The challenge in this phase is to build your brand.

- In the maturity phase, the seller's market gives way to a buyer's market. Margins decline as producers wrestle with each other

for a bigger slice of the pie. Marketers are challenged to revitalize their brands.

- During the phase of declining unit sales, marketers try to promote new uses for their old products, find new markets, or
  harvest as much profit as possible as the end draws near.

# 2

# Creating a Marketing Plan

## An Overview

## Key Topics Covered in This Chapter

- *The purpose of a marketing plan*

- *Planning the elements of the marketing mix*

- *Controlling the plan*

"**P**LAN YOUR WORK, and work your plan." That timeless piece of business philosophy can help you succeed in any number of workplace activities—including marketing. This chapter explains the marketing plan and its many elements.

## From Strategy to Plan

A *marketing plan* lays out a campaign that aims to fulfill a company's market strategy. At the business unit or product level, the plan aims to transform a product or service concept into a successful offering that meets the needs of target customers and fulfills the company's expectations for sales, market share, and so forth. The plan states exactly what the company will do in launching new products and supporting older ones. It indicates the timing of sales and promotional activities, pricing intentions, and distribution efforts. How the plan will be controlled and the results measured are also part of the plan. Plans are contained in binders and are treated with confidentiality lest competitors use their details to deploy counterefforts.

Most plans include the following (for the company or for a product line):

- **An executive summary.**

- **A table of contents.**

- **A summary of the current situation.** This contains all relevant data, including SWOT analysis (analysis of strengths, weaknesses, opportunities, and competitive threats).

- **A focused assessment of the market opportunity.** This includes a statement of target market segments, a customer and needs assessment, and the competitive challenges faced by the company and its products (or particular product line).

- **Financial and marketing goals.** Financial goals are usually expressed as incremental revenue improvements, and expected profits at the end of the planning period. Marketing goals are expressed as unit sales or market share.

- **A summary of the company's marketing strategy.** This summary identifies the target market and indicates how the product or product line will be positioned, distributed, and priced. It also enumerates the specific actions that will be taken to achieve the stated goals. Those actions may include reorganization of the sales force, the use of customer rebates, a national ad campaign, direct mail programs, and so forth.

- **A month-to-month marketing budget.**

- **Forecast month-to-month unit sales and revenues.**

- **A plan for monitoring and evaluating action plans in progress and at the end of the plan period.**

Note that the appendix contains a helpful marketing plan template that you can use to develop a plan that fits your company's unique requirements. Check it out.

## Implementing Your Plan via the Marketing Mix

The marketing plan begins with customer targeting, something we'll deal with in detail later. After the target customer segments have been identified, the plan addresses them through the *marketing mix*. The marketing mix—also called the four P's of marketing—includes product, place, price, and promotion (see figure 2-1). These represent the tools you will use to pursue your objectives in the target market.

(Note: Identifying the target market is an essential part of any marketing plan. So, too, is position. We discuss these important topics in chapter 4.)

## Product

The *product* (or service) is the centerpiece of the marketing mix. Whether it's a life insurance policy, a washing machine, or a broadband Internet service, the product is the company's offer to customers. That offer includes physical aspects as well as the less tangible elements, such as warranties, option choices, and after-sales service. Thus, the product is the entire package you offer to customers.

FIGURE 2-1

**Applying the marketing mix to a target market**

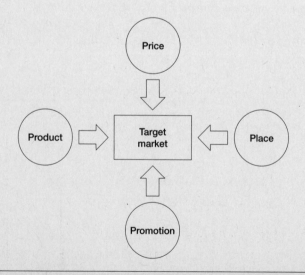

You can differentiate products physically or through the services your company provides in support of the product. Products' physical distinctions include the following:

- Form—size, shape, physical structure; for example, aspirin coating and dosage

- Features—for example, a word processing program's new text-editing tool

- Performance quality—the level at which the product's primary characteristics function

- Conformance quality—the degree to which all the units of the product perform equally

- Durability—the product's expected operating life under natural or stressful conditions

- Reliability—the probability that the product won't malfunction or fail

- Repairability—the ease with which the product can be fixed if it malfunctions

- Style—the product's look and feel

- Design—the way all the foregoing qualities work together (it's easy to use, looks nice, and lasts a long time)

You can also differentiate your product by service distinctions that set it apart. Service distinctions include the following:

- Ordering ease—how easy it is for customers to buy the product

- Delivery—how quickly and accurately the product is delivered

- Installation—how well the work is done to make the product usable in its intended location

- Customer training—whether your company offers to train customers in using the product

- Customer consulting—whether your company offers advice or research services to buyers

- Maintenance and repair—how well your company helps customers keep the product in good working order

The actual design of the product or service should be guided by a deep understanding of what customers need, want, and are willing to pay for, as determined by market understanding and research.

## Place

*Place* refers to the point of sale and the distribution of the product or service. Place may be a retail store, a national distributor network, an e-commerce Web site, or a direct mail catalog. Offering the product where and when customers want it is one of the most critical aspects of any marketing plan.

Witness the success of Amazon.com and Dell. Amazon.com made books and other items handily available to customers 24/7, and in a place that many found convenient—an Internet Web site. At a time when the book-buying public had to make time-consuming trips to a bricks-and-mortar bookstore and browse through thousands of on-shelf products, Amazon.com offered a less time-consuming alternative and far greater product selection. True, Amazon.com customers missed out on the pleasures of traditional bookstore browsing and had only limited opportunities to thumb through prospective purchases. But Amazon.com's "place" gave them something bookstores didn't provide: customer reviews and ratings.

Dell's is another story of "place" success. Its strategic decision to sell directly to customers gave it a leg up on competitors in the battle for personal computer sales. While rivals followed the traditional approach of distributing through retail stores and dealers, Dell skipped the middleman. Selling direct allowed Dell to do the following:

- Capture customer information that would otherwise be missed through other forms of distribution

- Practice made-to-order manufacturing, another differentiating factor in a product class where competing products are very similar

- Make its product available 24/7

Few companies use a single place for transacting business with customers. Many have *market channels* through which they meet customers; the more numerous and effective these channels are, the greater the opportunities to make sales. The publisher of this book, for example, will take advantage of several channels, as shown in figure 2-2. It will use a sales force to obtain shelf space in retail bookstores and will sell through Amazon.com. The sales force will also sell some copies to book wholesalers, which in turn will supply independent bookstores. Specialized employees of the publisher will pursue direct bulk sales with corporations and with book clubs. Meanwhile, a foreign rights specialist in the publisher's marketing department will attempt to sell translation rights for the book to non-English-language publishers around the world. The publisher will also use its e-commerce Web site to sell directly to final customers, avoiding the middlemen and the discounts they extract.

**FIGURE 2-2**

**Many paths to the customer**

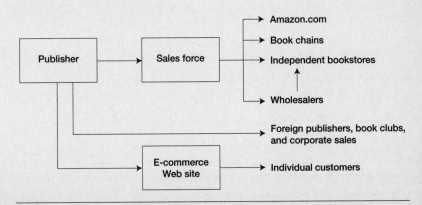

There are many paths to customers. A market-driven company takes as many of them as it can reasonably handle without causing conflicts between channels.

What aspects of "place" does your company use in its marketing plans? Are these the most optimal for satisfying customers and producing the sales and profits you seek, or are you simply following an old, unexamined blueprint for putting your product or service in front of customers? Think about it. Place is often taken for granted, but it makes a huge impact on marketing performance.

### Price

*Price* is what a buyer must give up in exchange for your product or service. Pricing in a competitive environment is both critical and challenging. If you set the price too low, you'll increase unit sales at the expense of profits. If you set it too high, some of your customers will walk into the waiting arms of competitors. Price decisions include price point, list price, discounts, payment period, and so on.

In free and competitive markets, pricing is the linchpin of most transactions. When a customer who wants a product perceives that its value is worth the asking price, a transaction will take place, barring other choices. Thus, moving the price higher or lower regulates the quantity of units sold. This point has implications for the product life cycle. You can price much more aggressively when your product is perceived as new, unique, and without strong substitutes, but you must often reduce your price as substitutes and competitors appear in the maturity stage of the cycle.

Generally, your flexibility in pricing is a function of the uniqueness of your product or service (see figure 2-3). This is because customers have difficulty in assessing the value of more unique offerings, such as a custom-built guitar or a fully restored 1962 MG sports car. There are few if any comparables, making valuation difficult. The exact opposite is true among commodity products, such as heating oil and electrical wiring. In these cases, sellers have little flexibility. If they price their offering higher than the going rate, sales will plummet. If they drop the price, sales will temporarily increase but will

**FIGURE 2-3**

**Pricing flexibility and product uniqueness**

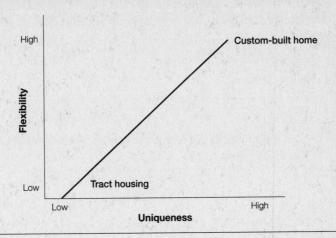

level off as competitors drop their prices—confounding the profitability of all sellers.

Some sellers successfully maintain a high price by surrounding their very ordinary products with an aura of uniqueness, quality, or exoticism. This approach is commonplace in, for example, the cosmetics industry.

Wherever you price your product or service, that price is an important element of the marketing mix and will have an impact on your results. You can price for any of the following objectives: to increase unit sales, profits, or market share; to undermine a competitor; or to keep competitors from entering your turf. Successful companies design their new products with specific price targets in mind. (Note: For more details on pricing, refer to chapter 9).

### Promotion

*Promotion*, the fourth element in the marketing mix, is the most difficult one to describe. It is all the communicative activities you use to ensure that customers know about your offerings, have a favorable impression of them, and actually make a transaction. These activities include advertising, catalogs, contests, public relations, and personal selling. Within these categories we have TV, radio, and print ads, billboards, product placements in movies, sponsorship of public TV and radio channels, two-for-one dinner specials, customer loyalty programs, telemarketing, direct mail sales, and door-to-door solicitations. And on and on.

The many faces of promotion are too numerous to cover in a book of this size. Suffice it to say that, along with market research, promotion provides the critical communication link between your company and the customers you aim to serve.

## Controlling Plan Implementation

Even when you're prepared with a cohesive plan, adequate resources, and all the right skills, you are bound to encounter surprises during implementation of your marketing plan. That's because business, like life, rarely plays out according to plan. Here are a few examples of the many surprises your firm may experience:

- Customer demand is lower than what your market research led you to believe.

- Consumers use your product in ways you never intended.

- A previously invisible competitor blindsides you with a dazzling new offering.

- The cost of an ad campaign is higher than you estimated.

Constant monitoring and control of the firm's marketing activities can help your company respond effectively to these kinds of unexpected events. Table 2-1 shows four types of marketing controls and explains who's responsible, why you might select a particular form of control, and how you might implement these control measures. Note that many items in the "How to control" column are quantitative metrics: expense-to-sales ratio, product territory profitability, and so forth. Metrics are like the gauges on an aircraft con-

**TABLE 2-1**

## Controlling your marketing plan

| Type of control | Who is responsible? | Why this control type? | How to control |
|---|---|---|---|
| Annual plan | Top and middle managers | To assess whether planned results have been achieved | Analyze sales, market share, marketing expense-to-sales ratio |
| Profitability | Marketing controllers | To see where the company is making and losing money | Measure profitability by product, territory, customer, segment, channel, order size; measure ROI |
| Efficiency | Line and staff managers; marketing controllers | To improve the spending and impact of marketing dollars | Measure efficiency of sales force, advertisements, sales promotions, distribution |
| Strategy | Top managers, marketing auditors | To ask whether the company is pursuing the best market, product, and channel opportunities | Review marketing effectiveness and company's social and ethical responsibilities |

*Source:* Harvard ManageMentor® on Marketing Essentials, adapted with permission.

trol panel, indicating where you are and showing key parameters of operating performance.

Depending on your role, you may find yourself responsible for one or more of these activities. Or others in your company may need your help in gathering the required information to conduct these assessments. Whichever part of the control process you're involved in, you can feel proud about contributing to a key stage in your firm's marketing campaign.

## Summing Up

- A marketing plan states exactly what the company will do in launching new products and supporting older ones. It indicates the timing of its sales and promotional activities, pricing

intentions, and distribution efforts. How the plan will be controlled and the results measured are also part of the plan.

- A marketing plan is based on customer targeting and the elements of the marketing mix: product (or service), place, price,
  and promotion (the four P's).

- Product is the company's offer to customers. It includes the
  physical aspects of the offer as well as intangible elements, such
  as warranties.

- Place refers to the point of sale and the distribution of the
  product or service. Place may be a retail store, a national distributor network, an e-commerce Web site, a direct mail catalog, or something else.

- Price is what a buyer must give up in exchange for the seller's
  product. In free and competitive markets it is a regulator of
  customer demand. Generally, sellers have greater flexibility in
  pricing when their offer is unique; they have less flexibility as
  their offers become commodity-like.

- Promotion describes the many communicative activities used to
  ensure that customers know about the company's offerings, have
  a favorable impression of them, and actually make a transaction.

# 3

# Market Research

*Listen and Learn*

## Key Topics Covered in This Chapter

- *Formal and informal methods of market research*

- *The research process*

- *Two methods for analyzing customer preferences*

I S YOUR BUSINESS doing well? Are its products and services popular with customers? If they are, that's good. But don't expect the good times to last forever. Customer preferences change. Competitors lure buyers away with new offerings, and customers perceive new needs that no one has yet addressed.

In business, long-term survival and growth result from the successful exploitation of new market opportunities. You find those opportunities by listening and learning. Listening and learning are essential organizational skills that, in the end, separate winners from losers. They are what companies must do to understand customers and competitors and to identify market opportunities. As you'll discover in this chapter, listening and learning take many forms.

In the past, the marketing function usually owned this job and pursued it through formal market research and analysis of customer data. We now recognize that this was a mistake; listening and learning are everyone's responsibility. Customers are always signaling their needs, preferences, likes, and dislikes, and everyone must make an effort to pick up on those signals. Formal marketing research is only one of many ways to do this. Salespeople have daily contact with customers; every contact is an opportunity to listen and learn. Product developers talk to *lead users*, who routinely alter off-the-shelf products to suit their unique needs. Service representatives get yet another glimpse into the minds of customers and their changing desires and requirements; more than anyone else, service reps can pinpoint customer dissatisfaction.

Yes, there are many ways to understand customers and identify market opportunities, and we'll describe some in this chapter. The challenge, of course, is to form a coherent picture from many pieces of learning. Customer knowledge and market understanding are like pieces of a jigsaw puzzle. Viewed in isolation, they tell us nothing. It's only when you begin to assemble the pieces that a meaningful picture emerges.

## Formal Market Research

*Market research* refers to the formal collection, analysis, and reporting of external data that a company finds relevant to its businesses. It is, in the words of Vincent Barabba and Gerald Zaltman, "the process of listening to the voice of the market and conveying information about it to appropriate management."[1] The point of that information is to make better decisions, as shown in the example of Tesco (see "Best Practice in Customer Data: Tesco"). Market research may be as simple as a customer comment card—or as complex as a nationwide sample survey that requires a thoughtful section of survey questions, randomized sampling techniques, and statistical analysis of the final data.

There are six main types of formal market research:

- **Direct observation.** Observe what customers are buying and how they use their purchases. Pay particular attention to the difficulties they experience in using popular products and services. Those difficulties may represent market opportunities. Salespeople are good partners in observational research. (Later in this chapter we'll explain a unique approach to observation called empathetic design.)

- **Experimentation.** A packaged-goods company will often introduce a new product at different prices or in different sized packages in a selected number of stores. Customer response is recorded. The price or package size is then changed, and the customer response to this change is tabulated. The insights gained through such experiments support decisions on rolling out products to broader markets.

## Best Practice in Customer Data: Tesco

Few companies have demonstrated as much ingenuity and skill at gathering and using customer purchase data as Tesco, a leading U.K. supermarket chain. By mining customer data collected through its Tesco loyalty card, it has gathered remarkable insights into customer needs, their satisfaction with existing products, and opportunities for new sales. The company has leveraged that information into the world's largest online grocery service and has used its Web site to launch the online sale of many nongrocery products, including books, CDs and DVDs, credit cards, loans, insurance, and mobile phone and broadband service. Customers can even use the Tesco Web site to compare and switch between U.K. vendors of heating gas and home electricity. Tesco's remarkable story is ably told by the consultants who helped make it happen in *Scoring Points* (for more information, see "For Further Reading").

- **Gathering and analysis of purchase data.** Computer technology and bar coding have made it possible for companies to keep tabs on customer behavior and preferences. Using point-of-sale scanning, for example, a supermarket can accurately and quickly determine customer preferences for different types and sizes of soft drinks. ScrubaDub, a Boston-area car wash chain, bar-codes customer vehicles; it uses the collected data to determine service preferences and frequency of use and to reward loyal customers. Direct mail companies like Lands' End go a step further; they mine their customer databases to determine which customers should receive special catalogs or offers.

- **Survey research.** Surveys are used to poll customers and potential customers on a broad array of issues: satisfaction, preferences, price resistance, knowledge of products and services, and so forth. A *sample survey* is used to query randomized samples of the larger population in a statistically valid way that ensures, within certain limits, that the results can be extrapolated to the larger (unsampled) part of the population.

- **Focus groups.** A *focus group* is a small group of invitees who, guided by a trained moderator, discuss a product, a service, their perceptions of a particular company, or even political issues. The moderator might ask focus group members, for example, "How do you feel about the rising price of gasoline?" "What do you think should be done by automakers to mitigate the negative effects of those rising prices?" "Which of the major automakers is most likely to deal effectively with the problem?"

- **Interviewing dissatisfied and lapsed customers.** No one likes bad news, but you can learn more from dissatisfied and lapsed customers than from anyone else. Potential customers can tell you what they want, but there is no assurance that they will reach for their wallets if you offer it. Satisfied customers can tell you what they like about your offer. But you probably already know what they like. Dissatisfied and lapsed customers, on the other hand, can point the finger at what stands between your products and services and much better sales.

You can obtain a great deal of market data through public sources: government publications, census data, trade magazines, trade shows, industry reports, and the Internet. Many small companies, lacking funds for stand-alone research departments, should avail themselves of these sources (see "The Research Process"). Still other research can be purchased from research services for a fee. For customized research, outside research firms can often fill the bill.

## Two Formal Methods for Analyzing Buyer Preferences

One of the most important chores of formal research is to analyze buyer preferences. Unless you understand what potential buyers prefer, you cannot have an effective product development operation or

## The Research Process

Market research is a seven-step process. Researchers and the intended users of the research should collaborate in each step as follows:

1. Be very clear about the problem that you are asking market research to solve. If you get this step wrong, the remaining steps will waste time and energy.

2. Determine the type of information needed to solve the problem you identified in step 1.

3. Select the most appropriate research tools for getting the information you need. You may need more than one.

4. Design your tools to fit the situation. For example, if a focus group is the best tool, determine which people you'll invite to participate, how you'll direct your inquiry, and so forth.

5. Apply your research tool with objectivity and integrity. Don't skew it to confirm a preconceived idea of the "right" data.

6. Analyze the data objectively.

7. Communicate your findings to the people who need it and who can apply it.

marketing campaign. Until recently, the best approach to determining preferences was concept testing. More recently, researchers have begun applying a more sophisticated tool: conjoint analysis. Even if you are not involved in market research, you may be a consumer of its output. So it pays to understand these two methods.

## Concept Testing

Concept testing presents potential buyers with an idea—say, for a new Middle Eastern restaurant. They are then asked to choose between five responses:

- I would definitely buy.

- I would probably buy.

- I might or might not buy.

- I would probably not buy.

- I would definitely not buy.

If the people in the study are fairly representative of people in the target market, their responses to this set of choices will tell you quite a bit about the viability of your idea. But you'd want to know more. For a nondurable service such as our Middle Eastern restaurant, we would seek a deeper understanding of demand by asking, "If this restaurant were located in Smithville, how often would you stop in? Once a week? Once a month? Once every few months?" And so forth.

Many products and services can be described as a bundle of attributes. For example, a restaurant has several attributes that matter to a greater or lesser extent to diners: food quality, menu variety, ambiance, service quality, convenient parking. Concept testing can help us understand the extent to which people in the target market value these different attributes. And once we know this, we can fine-tune the design and execution of the restaurant idea. You can obtain this information by using a questionnaire like the one shown in figure 3-1.

Finally, unless your product or service is entirely new, you can assume that your respondents are currently patronizing other vendors. In these cases it is useful to determine their current level of satisfaction with those competitors. High satisfaction will temper any stated willingness to try your product. Low satisfaction gives you some assurance that the respondent who testified to a high likelihood of

FIGURE 3-1

## A sample questionnaire

How important are the following restaurant factors to you?

|  | Very important |  |  |  | Not important |
|---|---|---|---|---|---|
| Food quality |  |  |  |  |  |
| Menu variety |  |  |  |  |  |
| Ambiance |  |  |  |  |  |
| Service quality |  |  |  |  |  |
| Ample parking |  |  |  |  |  |

trying your product or service will actually follow through. Satisfaction is generally measured with a simple questionnaire such as the one in figure 3-2.

Concept testing is not without weaknesses. If interviewees respond negatively to the idea, you cannot be sure how their response reflects trade-offs they've made between the components of the idea, and this makes it difficult to reformulate the idea into a more customer-pleasing package. You can overcome that weakness by using a more sophisticated tool: conjoint analysis.

FIGURE 3-2

## A simple questionnaire for measuring satisfaction

How satisfied are you with the restaurants located in your area?

| Very satisfied |  | Somewhat satisfied |  | Not at all satisfied |
|---|---|---|---|---|
|  |  |  |  |  |

## Conjoint Analysis

Many new products and services are complex bundles of attributes; customers are bound to place different values on those attributes. For example, the relevant attributes of telescopes used by amateur astronomers include the following:

- The aperture, or the diameter of the main lens or mirror (the larger the aperture, the greater its ability to capture light from dim objects)

- The optical quality (the ability of the optical system to separate objects)

- The quality of the mounting (the degree to which it prevents vibrations and enables flawless star tracking)

- The computer locating system (how well it directs the scope to specified coordinates on the celestial grid)

- The price

In a perfect world, telescope buyers would optimize each of these attributes for the same price. They'd order an instrument with the greatest aperture, the highest quality optical resolution, and the sturdiest and most sophisticated mounting, and they'd have it equipped with a computer drive that would take them to the sky coordinates they entered into the system.

Unfortunately, the world isn't perfect. Bigger and better costs more, forcing buyers to make trade-offs between attributes. For example, one buyer might skimp on aperture size in order to optimize optical quality. She might also put a higher value on a sturdy mounting at the expense of the computer guidance system, figuring that she could add that feature later, when her budget allowed.

It is difficult to think of a complex product or service—from hotels, resorts, and digital cameras, to banking and credit card services—for which customers do not have to make trade-offs between relevant attributes. *Conjoint analysis* is a statistical technique for predicting how they will make those trade-offs. Its objective is to determine what combination of a limited number of relevant attributes is most preferred by potential buyers. Market researchers find conjoint analysis useful in forecasting customer acceptance of new products and services.

Although each participant in a conjoint study will respond in an individual way, analysis will usually reveal which attributes have the greatest value and the *extent* to which various attributes are desired. At bottom, it clarifies the value system used by participants in making choices. Understanding that value system allows us to predict buyer choices.

The details of this powerful tool are beyond the scope of this book. Those details are usually attended to, in any case, by trained market researchers (although many software packages are now available for companies that lack research departments). However, the method generally involves these steps.

1. Select the relevant attributes of the product or service; it is crucial to get this step right. As in the telescope example, you must know which attributes matter to customers in this product category.

2. Show different attribute combinations to study participants (e.g., combo A is a single-family home with three bedrooms, two baths, a brick patio, and a two-car garage, at $350,000; combo B is a single-family home with two bedrooms, etc., at $275,000). Ideally, these combinations should be similar—close substitutes—but sufficiently different that participants will be able to discern and articulate a choice.

3. Ask participants to rank the various attribute combinations in terms of their individual preferences.

4. Apply statistical analysis of the participant responses (usually done with specialized software).

The resulting analysis indicates the utility of each attribute, as seen by potential buyers. You can then move forward with product or service development having confidence that its formulation will be accepted by the target market.

Note: Professor Robert Dolan of Harvard Business School has written a useful and nontechnical class note covering the working details of concept testing and conjoint analysis. It is listed in "For Further Reading."

## Understanding Customer Price Sensitivity

The price sensitivity of customers is one of the factors that market planners should understand. Market opportunities usually expand or shrivel as a function of price. Thus, whether you intend to offer customers a new banking service or a low-carbohydrate family of snack foods, or to seek a greater market share of an existing product, you must have an informed awareness of the relationship between price and demand.

A basic tenet of economics is that in a free market people will buy more of a good or service when the price goes down, and less as the price goes up, all other factors being constant. Some products and services have greater price elasticity than others. This is both intuitively obvious and easily substantiated.

Figure 3-3 shows the elasticity of demand for two products: A and B. The sharp slope in the demand curve (D) for product A indicates a high sensitivity to a price increase; customers will make many fewer purchases as the price increases. Product B, in contrast, demonstrates much less sensitivity to a price increase. These customers reduce their purchases only slightly in the face of rising prices; as economists would say, demand for product B is relatively inelastic.

Some goods and services, such as product B, demonstrate relatively low price sensitivity—at least in the short term. Consider automobile fuel. The 30 percent rise in U.S. gasoline prices in the fall of 2004, when crude oil skyrocketed to $54 per barrel, caused only a 2–3 percent drop in U.S. gasoline consumption. Why? People were so locked in to vacation plans and commuting routines that the increase caused little more than a ripple in demand. If that level of pricing (or rising prices) were to persist for a long time, however, consumption would drop substantially as people stopped buying

FIGURE 3-3

**Sensitivity to price**

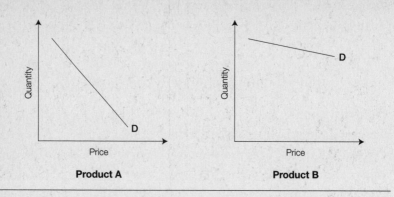

Product A                          Product B

gas-guzzling SUVs, opted to use public transportation, began car-pooling to work, and so forth.

As if to confirm this long-term effect, OPEC, the cartel of oil-producing countries, intimated that it wanted to see crude prices return to the $32–$35 per barrel range. Although the spurt in prices was a huge windfall for OPEC members, they knew that sustained high prices would induce their customers to find substitutes for petroleum and to invest seriously in alternative energy sources—hurting oil producers in the long run.

Like product A, many products and services exhibit a much more immediate and dramatic response to price changes, usually because the product or service is nonessential or because it has many available substitutes. Beef is an example. Every time the price of beef has increased sharply, demand has declined immediately and sometimes dramatically. Shoppers look at the price and say, "I think we'll have chicken for dinner tonight."

Economists use the term *price elasticity of demand* to quantify the impact of price changes on customer demand. If you've taken microeconomics, you are probably familiar with this concept. Price elasticity of demand is calculated as follows:

Percentage change in quantity / Percentage change in price =
Price elasticity of demand

Thus, if a company raised the price of a product from $100 to $120, price would increase by 20 percent. If that increase caused the quantity sold to drop from 600 units to 550 units, the percentage decrease would be 8.3 percent. Following our formula, the price elasticity of demand would be

8.3/20 = 0.42 (Any value under 1 is considered "inelastic")

The higher the final number, the more sensitive customers are to price changes. Any value under 1 is considered inelastic, and any value over 1 is considered elastic. For the elasticity of many commonplace goods and services, see the table on this Web site: www.mackinac.org/article.asp?ID=1247.

Often you can determine how customers will respond to a price change through focus groups, questionnaires, and direct experiments in local markets. For example, the producer of a breakfast cereal sold throughout the EU might raise its price in Brussels and observe the impact on unit sales.

To complete this analysis, however, the strategist should calculate the anticipated impact of a price change on total revenue. People may be buying fewer items at a higher price. For the example given in the formula, the company had been selling 600 units at $100 each, earning revenues of $60,000. Under its new scenario, it expects to sell 550 units at $120, resulting in total revenue of $66,000. Further analysis would be needed to determine whether that higher revenue figure will translate into higher or lower gross profits.

Formal studies of price elasticity of demand are normally reserved for tactical market moves. Nevertheless, understanding the relationship between price levels and customer buying behavior is an important piece of the larger puzzle that market planners must understand.

How well do you understand customer price sensitivity in your markets? How does that understanding inform your strategic choices?

## Informal Research Methods:
## Close Customer Contact

Traditional market research methods produce useful results when the steps of the research process are scrupulously observed and personal bias is not allowed to creep in. But this arms-length objectivity—or "peopleproofing"—can create a barrier to learning what customers really think and feel, and to accessing what may be excellent ideas for product or service innovation. It's described by Vincent Barabba, one of the masters of effective market research:

> People proofing is a deliberate effort to minimize human bias in experimental design, sampling procedures, the construction and administration of questionnaires, and many other things that data gathering involves. Unfortunately . . . people proofing also screens out the benefits of imagination, creativity, and personal insights—the very qualities that contribute to the development of breakthrough products and services.[2]

To avoid screening out those benefits, some companies are turning to nontraditional means of market research. These include learning from leader users, empathetic design, and immersion.

### Learning from Lead Users

A valuable source of innovative ideas, *lead users* are companies and individuals—customers and noncustomers—whose needs are far ahead of market trends. They may be pioneering radiologists searching for better methods of producing or interpreting scanned images. They may be military pilots, professional athletes, or engineers who have discovered ways of modifying off-the-shelf equipment for substantially greater effectiveness in the field. In all cases, the needs of lead users motivate them to produce innovations that suit their unique requirements—often before manufacturers think of them.

Lead users are seldom interested in commercializing their ideas or practices. Instead, they innovate for their own purposes because existing products fail to meet their needs. Their innovations can often be adapted, however, to the needs of larger markets that will be recognized many months or years in the future.

MIT professor Eric von Hippel was the first to study lead users as a source for innovative ideas. In several of the fields he studied—notably scientific instruments, semiconductors, and computers—more than half of all innovations were made by users, not by manufacturers. Thus, approaching these lead users and studying their unique applications and product modifications can provide valuable insights for future products and services (see "A Four-Phase Process for Capturing the Ideas of Lead Users"). For example, von Hippel suggests that an automotive brake manufacturer might seek out particular users whose requirements for effective braking exceed those of typical users. These might be auto-racing teams, producers of military aircraft, or manufacturers of heavy trucks.

### Empathetic Design

One of the problems faced by market researchers and their companies is that target customers cannot always recognize or articulate their future needs. Could you have imagined an MP3 player back in 1995? Would you have told a market researcher in 1990 that you wanted an automobile with a hybrid gasoline–electric engine?

Because most people are not aware of technical possibilities, they tend to identify their needs in terms of current products and services with which they are familiar. They express their needs in terms of incremental improvements to these existing products and services: a thinner laptop, an automobile with better fuel economy, a TV screen with better resolution, faster mail delivery service. Empathetic design is a technique for identifying these unrecognized needs.

*Empathetic design* is a technique whereby researchers observe how people use existing products and services in their own environments. Harley-Davidson used this technique when it sent engineers, marketing personnel, and even social anthropologists to HOG (Harley Owners Group) events. These employees observed how Harley owners used and customized their motorcycles, the problems they encountered, and so forth. Those observations became the raw materials for marketing and new-product decisions.

Following this same strategy, a Japanese consumer electronics company sent a young engineer to live with an American family for six months; his mission was to observe how family members cooked their meals, communicated with friends, and entertained themselves. Those observations were used to create new electronic consumer products.

## A Four-Phase Process for Capturing the Ideas of Lead Users

An article coauthored by Eric von Hippel, Stefan Thomke, and Mary Sonnack described a four-phase process used by some 3M units to glean innovative ideas from lead users. This process may work for you.

1. **Lay the foundation.** Identify the targeted markets and the type and level of innovations desired by your organization's key stakeholders.

2. **Determine the trends.** Talk to experts in the field about what they see as the important trends. These experts should have a broad view of emerging technologies and leading-edge applications in the area being studied.

3. **Identify and learn from the lead users.** Use networking to identify users at the leading edge of the target market and related markets. Develop relationships with these lead users, and gather information from them that points to promising ideas that could contribute to breakthrough products. Use what you learn to shape preliminary product ideas and assess their business potential.

4. **Develop breakthroughs.** The goal of this phase is to move preliminary concepts toward completion. Host two- or three-day workshops with several lead users, a small group of in-house marketing and technical people, and the lead user investigative team. Work in small groups and then as a whole to design final concepts.

SOURCE: Adapted from Eric von Hippel, Stefan Thomke, and Mary Sonnack, "Creating Breakthroughs at 3M," *Harvard Business Review*, September–October 1999, 47–57.

Some companies take this approach very seriously. IDEO, a leading product design company, bases its design process on an anthropologic approach. Procter & Gamble, a prolific maker of new products, is another. It trains all new R&D personnel in what it calls "product research," the P&G approach to observing how customers use products day-to-day. The goal is to put people who have knowledge of technical possibilities and design in direct contact with the world experienced by potential customers.

As described by Dorothy Leonard and Jeffrey Rayport, empathetic design is a five-step process:[3]

1. **Observe.** As described earlier, company representatives observe people using products in their homes and workplaces. The key questions in this step are, who should be observed, and who should do the observing?

2. **Capture data.** Observers should capture data on what people are doing, why they are doing it, and the problems they encounter. Because much of the data is visual and unquantifiable, use photographs, videos, and drawings to capture the data.

3. **Reflect and analyze.** In this step, observers return from the field and share their experiences with colleagues. Reflection and analysis may result in returning people to the field for more observations.

4. **Brainstorm.** This step is used to transform observations into graphical representations of possible solutions.

5. **Develop solution prototypes.** Prototypes clarify new concepts, allow others to interact with them, and can be used to provoke the reactions and comments of potential customers. Are potential customers attracted by the prototypes? What alterations do they suggest?

As you can well imagine, empathetic design is critical when you're developing consumer products for overseas markets, where preferences for product sizes, colors, and applications may be quite different from those found in the home market.

## Immersion

In their fine little book *Simply Better*, Patrick Barwise and Seán Meehan use spy writer John le Carré's warning—"A desk is a dangerous place from which to watch the world"—to remind executives to get out of their offices and immerse themselves in the world of customers and competitors. But simply getting out there is not enough. The authors cite research showing that CEOs of high-performing and low-performing companies spend roughly the same amount of time with customers (18 percent and 15 percent, respectively), but there is a qualitative difference in how these leaders spend their time.

> The CEOs of the low performers spent much of their time with customers socializing at cultural or sporting events. While entertaining may help solidify some relationships, it does not present a good context for useful customer feedback. CEOs of high performers, on the other hand, were less interested in such socializing; they wanted to get down to business and, especially, to know how their company was performing relative to its promises and the customer's expectations. They also persistently asked their customers how they could do better.[4]

Immersion by key people is important, but particularly so for high-ranking decision makers, for the simple reason that they can get the organization to respond. Executives don't like being told, "Your product is inferior to what we can buy elsewhere cheaper." And they don't like hearing, "It takes over an hour to get someone in your customer service center to even talk to us." They are embarrassed to the point of doing something about it. If a sales rep reported those comments, management might brush them off: "That sounds like an excuse for not getting the order." Or the sales rep's report might go into a complaint file and not be acted on for months—if at all.

Executive "immersees" should be particularly alert to customer dissatisfaction—not solely with their own product and service, but also with the category in general. "All of these products are (too heavy, too expensive, difficult to use, impossible to adjust, etc)." Category dissatisfaction can be a key indicator of market opportunity. For more on this, see "Tips for Making Your Workforce Outward-Looking."

Note: One of the important goals of market research is to determine what customers value. What results do they want? How do they want the results delivered? What price are they willing to pay for the results they seek? If you and your colleagues would like a

## Tips for Making Your Workforce Outward-Looking

Although marketing usually has the formal responsibility of actively seeking new market opportunities, everyone in the market-oriented company should be "outward-looking." The reason is that people with different training and experience are likely to catch something that others—such as marketing professionals—would miss. Here are a few ways to keep your people in touch with the external world of customers, competitors, and change:

- Send technical people to scientific, technology, and customer conferences.

- Create a small team of technical people and give them the part-time chore of scanning the literature and industry news for technical developments that might either threaten or provide opportunities for your business.

- Regularly sit in the customer call center.

- Start an informal luncheon to which academics and other experts are invited to talk about trends and new developments.

- Send executives and non–sales managers on customer calls with field reps. They can learn more about customers and competitors from doing this than from a stack of research reports.

"thinking tool" to explore these questions, turn to the "Calculating the Value of a Customer" worksheet in the appendix.

We have now examined two general ways of understanding customers and finding market opportunities: formal research and informal methods that bring you into close contact with customers. Which is better? Actually, better is not the issue, and choosing between them is not a solution. Experienced marketers know that they must do both, because each approach delivers an indispensable quality of understanding. Executives and managers can read market reports by the basketful, but they will make better decisions if they also develop a more visceral and empathetic sense of what customers are seeking.

## Summing Up

- Market research is a process for listening and learning, with the goal of making better decisions.

- Formal research includes direct observations, experimentation, the gathering and analysis of purchase data, customer surveys, focus groups, and contacts with dissatisfied and lapsed customers.

- Concept testing and conjoint analysis are formal methods for analyzing buyer preferences.

- The price elasticity of demand technique quantifies the impact of price changes on customer demands. Marketers need to understand the impact that price has on demand.

- Lead users are companies and individuals whose needs are far ahead of market trends. By observing them, marketers can develop ideas for innovative new products and services.

- Empathetic design gives researchers an opportunity to understand how people actually use products and services.

- Decision makers who directly hear customer wants or complaints are much more likely to respond to them than do those who experience customer issues indirectly through research reports.

# 4

# Market Customization

*Segmentation, Targeting, and Positioning*

## Key Topics Covered in This Chapter

- *Gaining focus through market segmentation*

- *The basics of multifactor, relevant, and effective segmentation*

- *Targeting the right segments*

- *Positioning the product or service in the minds of customers*

ARLY IN THE twentieth century, producers in the industrial economies of Europe and North America faced high, undifferentiated demand for manufactured goods, and relatively few competitors. For many product categories it was a mass market, and sellers satisfied it with high volumes of standardized goods. Perhaps the classic example was Ford's Model T automobile, identical versions of which were cranked out by the millions for a car-crazy society. Henry Ford famously remarked that customers could buy the Model T in any color they wished—as long as it was black.

Greater competition and more demanding customers have largely ended the era of mass marketing in many product categories. They have spurred producers to differentiate their products in ways that meet the unique needs of smaller customer groups, or market segments. Ford's standard black Model Ts gave way in the late 1920s to General Motors' strategy of producing different models to accommodate different pocketbooks, with the Chevrolet at the bottom and the Cadillac at the top.

The move away from mass marketing has affected almost every industry. If you need convincing, take a look at the pet food section of your local supermarket. Whereas individual pet food producers once offered only one type of dry cat food, they now offer many. You have your choice of standard and special formulations—for kittens, adult cats, elderly cats, overweight cats, cats subject to hairballs, and cats with kidney problems. Among the canned cat foods, each producer now offers at least ten flavors.

The upshot of the trend away from mass marketing is that companies are seeking to identify the unique needs and preferences of customers in ever smaller segments. If this strategy were carried to its logical conclusion—something that would be counterproductive in most industries—companies would design and produce goods and services for individual customers.

Generally, you'll find most companies operating along the continuum between the extremes of mass production and "markets of one." For example, Dell will build a computer customized to your specifications within a fairly broad range of components and software. Peachtree accounting software has special versions for manufacturers, retailers, and nonprofit businesses. Automakers allow you to order your new vehicle in the color you want and with the set of options you prefer (within limits), and they are working toward the day when you will be able to do all this online and have the new automobile delivered to your door in a few weeks.

Among manufacturers, this customizing capability is a function of advances in flexible manufacturing and modular product design and generally goes under the term *mass customization,* a production approach that uses those advances to create goods and services that meet the unique needs of specific customers. As described by B. Joseph Pine II in his landmark book on the subject, mass customization is the production of individually customized goods and services at mass production prices.[1] In reality, true market-of-one producers are relatively few: the personal fitness trainer, the local tailor who makes you a suit from scratch, the business consultant who works closely with you to help you develop an online e-commerce site that meets your unique requirements.

The same forces that push companies along the continuum from mass market to market-of-one require that they think deeply about segmentation, targeting, and positioning, the tools of the trade described in this chapter.

# Segmentation

*Segmentation* is a practice that seeks out pieces of the total market that contain customers with identifiable characteristics, as defined by income, age, personal interests, ethnic background, special needs, and so forth. The point of segmentation is to break a mass market into submarkets of customers who have common needs. Identifying these segments makes it possible to do two things: (1) create goods and services that are better tailored to the needs of specific customers and (2) focus marketing resources more efficiently.

The unsolicited seminar invitation you received in the mail today from a retirement planning firm you never heard of is one example of segmenting in action. You were in the pool of people to receive that invitation because a database determined that you have one or more of the following characteristics:

- You have assets (as indicated by the property tax rolls of your community).

- You are in the age group of people who should be thinking about retirement.

- You live in or near the community where the seminar will be held.

These characteristics have put you into a segment of interest to the retirement planners, who believe that their direct mail exhortation ("Let our experts help you plan your future!") has a chance to produce a response from you and people like you. Obviously, they want to focus their marketing resources on a group of people who are likely to have an interest in what they have to offer *and* the financial capacity to act.

Conceptually, the point of segmentation is obvious. It's not what you'd call rocket science. But below the conceptual level—at the level where the actual searching and sifting go on—it gets more complicated. There are plenty of ways to segment markets, as shown in table 4-1. Of these, demographics, behavior or interests, and affil-

**TABLE 4-1**

## Segmenting markets

| Demographics | Behavior or interests | Affiliation or occupation |
|---|---|---|
| Age | Golfers | Members of the armed forces |
| Gender | Wine aficionados | Teachers |
| Income | Pet owners | Republicans |
| Ethnic groups | Recent homebuyers | Farmers |

iation or occupation are often the most productive. Even though people may not always define themselves in these categories, being part of a category can tell the marketer something about their needs, spending proclivities, and spending capacities.

### Multifactor Segmentation

Naturally, one-dimensional labels such as "golfer" or "recent home-buyer" seldom tell a marketer enough to understand people or their needs. A great deal of complexity is missed. A golfer, for example, may be male or female, age sixteen with an annual income of $800 or age fifty-six with an annual income of $180,000. Consequently, the marketer must sift through the golfing population in terms of other characteristics to find the subsegment to which he or she can target a businesslike offer.

Consider figure 4-1, where the golfing population of the country is segmented in terms of three factors: annual income, gender, and age. Depending on the nature of the marketer's business and on previous research on the golfing population, she may determine that the two shaded segments in the figure—men aged 50–70 with annual incomes greater than $50,000—are the segments of greatest interest to her company, which manufactures sportswear.

Her initial research may indicate, for example, that people in these segments are the largest spenders on men's golfing apparel.

FIGURE 4-1

**Multifactor golfing segments**

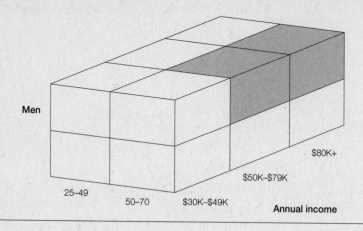

Men

25–49

50–70

$30K–$49K

$50K–$79K

$80K+

Annual income

This fact should spur the marketer to do more research on these specific segments. The sportswear company might, for example, use
focus groups to determine which particular clothing items would
appeal to male golfers in these age and income groups. Indeed, a
great deal must be learned about the different segments in terms of
their buying power, their product or service preferences, and their
attractiveness as potential market targets.

### Relevant and Effective Segmenting

Once you understand segmentation, you'll be in a better position to
concentrate your resources. But not all definable segments are relevant. For example, if your business produces fluorescent lightbulbs,
there is not much point in segmenting the total market by gender,
income, education, political affiliations, or most other characteristics. None of those characteristics is relevant to the purchase and use
of lightbulbs. Commercial use versus residential use might be the
most relevant approach to segmenting for this market.

Beyond relevance, there is the issue of effectiveness. Philip Kotler suggests that to be effective and useful to your business, a market segment must have certain characteristics.[2] It must be

- **Measurable.** You need to know its size, key characteristics, purchasing power, and preferences.

- **Substantial.** The segment of interest must be large enough to be profitably served by you.

- **Accessible.** There is no point in segmenting if you know in advance that there is no practical way to access a segment's members.

- **Differentiable.** Segments must respond differently to different marketing programs. Kotler gives the example of married and unmarried women's response to perfumes. If there is no difference in their responses, then there is no effective segmentation.

- **Actionable.** There must be a practical and cost-effective way to attract and serve customers in the segment.

### Segmenting Business Markets

Companies whose business is to serve other businesses—and not individual consumers—also segment their markets. In some cases they go beyond simply identifying relevant and effective segments. For example, the marketing departments of large banks are very interested in the owners and managers of small to midsized businesses, to whom they can sell trust services, cash management services, retirement plans, and commercial loans. Banks actually organize their operations to better focus their offers and delivery to these customers.

Segmenting, as noted earlier, lets you do a better job of tailoring products and services to the specific requirements of a group of customers. That's a good thing. But remember that focusing on narrow segments inevitably reduces the number of people for whom your offering will represent value. Keep this trade-off in mind.

## From Segmentation to Targeting

Once you understand the populations, behaviors, and profit potential of different market segments, you must target the ones that represent the greatest potential. But what is the basis for this targeting? There are many, including the following.

THE NUMBER OF CUSTOMERS IN THE SEGMENT AND THEIR TOTAL SPENDING POTENTIAL. Considering the costs of marketing and sales fulfillment, the segment should contain enough individuals with enough spending power to make the effort worthwhile. Ideally, the people in the segment will be heavy users of whatever you aim to sell. Better still, the number of potential buyers in the segment should be growing.

YOUR ABILITY TO REACH CUSTOMERS IN THE SEGMENT—AND THE COST OF DOING SO. A segment is not attractive if its members are difficult to reach or if the cost of doing so is prohibitive. Members of private golf courses are an ideal segment for retail investment management companies. These people typically have plenty of money for investments and discretionary spending. But reaching them is another story, because these clubs protect the privacy of their members. Similarly, a business book publisher figured that readers of the *Wall Street Journal* would be a perfect segment to target. However, the cost of ad space in the *Journal* relative to actual responses and sales revenues was such that this segment proved unattractive, at least through advertising.

THE INTENSITY OF EXISTING COMPETITION IN THE SEGMENT. Late-entry firms often discover that the segments with the greatest overall profit potential have already been targeted by an army of competitors. Some of these vendors may be well entrenched.

**THE LEVEL OF CUSTOMERS' SATISFACTION WITH COMPETITORS' CURRENT OFFERINGS.** Even when a segment bristles with competitors, research may reveal that customers are dissatisfied with current offerings and would welcome something different. On the other hand, if the satisfaction level is high, you should have second thoughts about targeting the segment. What you're looking for is a high likelihood of a positive response.

**FORECASTED GROWTH.** Is the segment forecasted to grow in size and spending power, or is it stagnant? You should consider not only the current situation but also the trend. For example, in early 2005 the U.S. population of hybrid-engine vehicles was only about 400,000—small by the standards of the industry. But that number was expected to grow rapidly in the following years. Anyone contemplating a marketing campaign to this market segment—perhaps for parts or after-sale service—would want to know the dimensions of that growth.

**POTENTIAL PROFITABILITY.** This is the bottom line of each of the preceding bases of segment targeting. You must estimate the profit potential, net of costs, of addressing a particular segment, as well as the likely direction of profit potential in the years ahead.

**BARRIERS TO ENTRY.** What are the entry barriers to a particular segment for you and for likely new competitors? Obviously, if barriers are low, there is little to stop other opportunistic firms from invading the segment—and driving down profitability.

Clearly, there is much to consider in targeting particular market segments, and you should proceed with caution. Segmenting allows you to concentrate scarce marketing resources and gives you opportunities to understand your customers at a level seldom available to mass marketers. For business-to-business vendors, there is no mass-market opportunity in any case; they must target defined segments.

The downside of segmenting, of course, is that it limits the number of potential customers who will learn about your product or service. It also ties the future of your product line to the fortunes of a particular segment. Growth may decline in that segment, taking your sales down with it. Customer preferences may change sharply, leaving your company holding an empty bag. So approach segmentation with a great deal of thought and caution. And if you're considering marketing to specific individuals, see "Are Micro-Segments the Next Big Thing?"

## Positioning

Once you've completed the related tasks of segmenting and targeting, you must develop a plan for your product or product line. As described in chapter 3, a marketing plan should engage each of the four P's: product, place, price, and promotion. Among the objects of

### Are Micro-Segments the Next Big Thing?

The emergence of powerful databases has raised expectations that the day is near when many companies will be able to directly target and serve individual customers on a one-to-one, "as you like it" basis. With computers now able to capture abundant purchasing information from individuals, analysis should make it possible to observe buying patterns, understand preferences, and then pursue sales to individuals through a strategy of micro-segment marketing. Some companies already do this. Hotel chains like Four Seasons, for example, keep track of guest preferences: how they like their morning coffee, which daily newspaper they prefer in the morning, and so forth.

Nevertheless, the day of micro-segment marketing appears to be no closer to reality than it did at the turn of this century. One reason may be that people do not want relationships with faceless corporations that exist solely to sell them things. And consumers resent Big Brother collecting information about them and using it to push products and services on them.

the plan is to position the product or service in the minds of potential customers.

*Positioning* is an attempt to manage how potential customers perceive a product or service. (It's really an aspect of differentiation, which we'll cover in detail later.) Volvo, for example, positions its vehicles in terms of durability and safety. Apple positions its products as elegant in design and user friendly. Vanguard Group mutual funds are positioned as well-managed funds with the lowest transaction costs.

The goal of positioning is to underscore one or two characteristics that make the product or service stand out in the minds of customers. Nirvana comes for the marketer when positioning takes the form of a slogan that sticks in the minds of customers. Consider the following:

Great taste!

It's good for your health.

Instant relief.

The best value for your money.

Reliability you can count on.

Safe and effective.

Built to last.

For young-looking hair.

State-of-the-art engineering at your fingertips.

Long-lasting.

Some positioning slogans stick in the public consciousness for decades. Consider Zenith Radio's 1927 slogan "The quality goes in before the name goes on." Or Timex's famous "It takes a licking and keeps on ticking." Or Ivory soap's "99 44/100% pure." Or Quaker Oatmeal's "It's the right thing to do." If you can get one of these positioning slogans into the public vocabulary, it may persist under its own power for decades.

Positioning should be the consequence of market research and a great deal of thought. It's one of those things you want to get right the first time, because *re*positioning is expensive and causes a great deal of confusion in the minds of customers. Once you decide on a position strategy, you should then apply resources through the marketing plan with the goal of implanting and reinforcing that positioning concept in the minds of customers.

One caveat: trying to position your product in a mental space occupied by a strong incumbent often ends in failure. Al Ries and Jack Trout, who literally wrote the book on positioning, refer to this as the Law of Exclusivity, stating, "When a competitor owns a word or position in the prospect's mind, it is futile to attempt to own the same word."[3] Thus, no one has been able to budge the public perception of Volvo as the "safe" car, or Duracell as the "long-lasting" battery. Ries and Trout's caveat assumes that customers can maintain only a single-dimensional mental fix on a product or service; in practical terms this means that only one brand can stand for one thing. This may represent an advertising person's view of buyer behavior, however, and may not rise to the level of an immutable law.

Take a minute to think about how your product or service is positioned—if it is positioned at all. Have you found a word or phrase that plants it firmly in the minds of customers in a positive or attractive way? Are you trying to position yourself in the same winner-takes-all space occupied by a competitor—and losing the battle?

Segmentation, targeting, and positioning—these three marketing tools usually work together. But be careful. Don't get too excited about them; segmenting and targeting narrow the market and limit your potential sales. Positioning assumes that customers are interested in only one thing, but reality may indicate that they are not. If you are truly customer focused, there will be times when segmenting is inappropriate and when positioning is self-defeating. So keep an open mind about these concepts.

## Summing Up

- Segmentation aims to break a mass market into submarkets of customers who have common needs. Successful segmenting allows a firm to focus its resources and to create goods and services that better meet customer needs.

- Demographics, behavior, interests, and affiliation or occupation are among the usual bases of segmentation.

- In many cases multifactor segmentation is called for—for example, not just homeowners, but high-income female homeowners.

- Once a market is segmented into relevant submarkets, you must identify those that have the greatest profit potential. Total spending potential, accessibility, and the intensity of competition in the segments are among the bases for targeting some segments and not others.

- Positioning is an attempt to manage how potential customers perceive a product or service. For example, Quaker Oatmeal ("It's the right thing to do") is positioned as the smart and healthy choice among breakfast cereals.

# 5

# Competitor Analysis

*Understand Your Opponents*

## Key Topics Covered in This Chapter

- *Identifying competitors*

- *Sizing up competitors*

- *Understanding the five forces that make markets attractive or unattractive*

As GEORGE DAY, a professor at the Wharton School, has perceptively written, "One of the primary issues facing managers in formulating competitive strategy is defining the arena of competition. Where are you competing? Who are your competitors? How attractive is the competitive arena?"[1] No effective marketing program is complete without a thoughtful analysis of competitors and the competitive arena.

You surely know who your competitors are. They are the ones your salespeople wrestle with every day in closing key sales. They are the companies that aim to steal your best customers. Yes, you know who they are, but how much do you know *about* them—their strengths and weaknesses? Some are ready and able to pounce on you if you invade a market segment they dominate; others will act slowly and perhaps ineffectually. Are you aware of emerging arenas of competition? And what about the competitors who will appear in the months and years ahead?

Some arenas of competition are relatively static, particularly in mature, capital-intensive industries. Before the 1970s, the steel industry could be defined as static. A handful of large competitors were slugging it out, each trying to lower unit production costs and capture a larger slice of the market at the expense of its rivals. This situation changed dramatically with the appearance of offshore producers and the rise of "mini-mills."

Other industries are more dynamic. Entertainment is a prime example. Fifty years ago, people in the United States had limited options for entertainment: three or four network television stations, a public television station, and one or two local stations, along with movie theaters and live performances. Today, TV viewers can still watch network channels, but they can also access hundreds of cable channels. The movie theaters are still there, but thousands of movies are now available through VHS, DVD, cable, and pay-per-view outlets. Because many of these entertainment services are vulnerable to substitution by others, vendors are scratching their heads and asking, "What strategy will help us carve out a profitable niche in this dynamic marketplace? And what's coming next that might render our product obsolete?"

A dynamic market has these hallmarks:

- Numerous products and services addressing a similar need (e.g., land line phones, cell phones, Internet phone service, instant messaging, e-mail)

- A diversity of competitors (e.g., TV networks, cable companies, video rental shops, live venues)

- Few insurmountable barriers to entry

- Market fragmentation

How well do you understand the competition in the market you aim to serve? Few areas of research provide greater dividends for the business strategist than this one. This chapter will help you assess the competition.

## Who Are Your Competitors?

The starting point of competitive analysis is the identification of your competitors. Who are they? If that question seems simpleminded, remember that your real competition—the ones that can kill your business—may not come from the handful of established companies you wrestle with every day. It may come instead from an unanticipated source.

If you doubt that, consider the photographic imaging business of twenty years ago. Camera makers such as Minolta, Canon, Olympus, and Nikon were busily fighting each other for the various segments of the picture-taking market. On the photo materials side, giants Kodak and Fuji were contending with each other for the sale of film, paper, and processing. All contenders understood the universe of competition.

Enter Sony in the early 1980s. Sony, a consumer electronics company better known for its radios, TVs, Walkman cassette players, and core competencies in microelectronics, unveiled the first consumer camera based on digital imaging. Twenty years later, digital cameras have upset the competitive applecart of the industry. Suddenly, newcomers like Hewlett-Packard, Gateway, and Casio—electronics companies like Sony—are players in a market once dominated by firms that understood optics and light-sensitive coated film. The point here is that when you think about competitors, you must recognize that you have both existing *and* potential competitors.

How do you identify your firm's main potential and existing competitors? Here's an easy rule of thumb: a *competitor* is any company that aims to satisfy the same customer needs that you do. This means that you must consider companies that offer substitutes for your products or services. For example, suppose you sell word-processing software. Your customer's need isn't for software, but for the ability to create documents quickly and conveniently. That need can be satisfied in many different ways: by pencils, pens, typewriters, "slate" PCs, and any other writing tool that innovative enterprises can dream up. Thus your company actually has more competitors than you might think.

Similarly, a manufacturer of photocopying machines aims to satisfy the need to duplicate documents. But a firm that offers document-duplicating *services*, such as Kinkos or the independent print shop down the street, may satisfy that need just as well. The service company is just as much your competitor as is another manufacturer of photocopy machines.

As you list your competitors, consider the following:

- Other players offering products similar to yours

- Companies that make substitutes for your products

- The ease with which customers comparison-shop and switch suppliers

- Your own suppliers' ability to raise their prices or reduce the quantity of their offerings

## Characteristics for Analysis

Once you've identified your potential and existing competitors, analyze them in terms of their ability to capture parts of the market.

### Strategies and Objectives

Your competitors may be following different strategies and pursuing different objectives. Consider this example.

*The strategy of company A, an investment management company, is to provide a full range of services for high-net-worth clients: financial planning, retirement planning, tax planning and preparation, insurance, and portfolio management. It aims to establish long-term client relationships with a small but wealthy pool of customers. Rival company B, on the other hand, is transaction oriented. It aims to be the low-cost provider of similar services, but for a wider market of customers. Its strategy is based on selling a high volume of computer-generated financial plans for less than $200.*

Also consider objectives. What objectives are your competitors pursuing? Profit maximization? Dominant market share? Is a competitor trying to break out of the segment it currently occupies and move into others? If these objectives are much different from yours, you may not need to worry about them. Your company may have effectively divided the market. But if competitors' objectives put them in head-to-head competition with you, you must either pre-pare yourself for a slugfest, find a way to differentiate your offer, or move into another market segment.

## Positioning

Usually, competitors in a market position themselves differently, both in terms of the segments they address and how they try to be perceived by customers. Figure 5-1 is a positioning map of the market for men's watches. It indicates roughly how the leading brands have positioned themselves in terms of two dimensions: sporty ver-sus fashion, and upscale precision versus affordable.

Creating a similar map for your own industry will give you a better idea of the competition and will show where each company concentrates its product development and marketing efforts. For good measure, ask knowledgeable associates to go through the same exercise, and then compare results.

FIGURE 5-1

**Competitor positioning, men's watches**

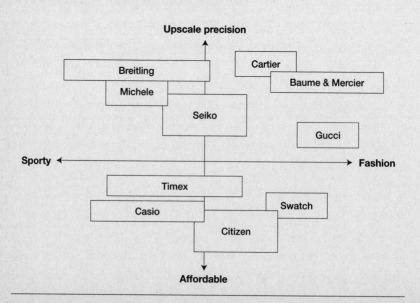

## Strengths and Weaknesses

Some companies have great products and prices but poor distribution. Others have great distribution but lackluster products. And then there are the competitors you should fear most: the ones who are strong in many areas. As you inventory your competition, make a systematic list of relative strengths like the one in table 5-1.

You can obtain such ratings through a brainstorming session among company personnel—in particular, the marketing manager, experienced salespeople, and customer service employees. Employee views on strengths and weaknesses may lack objectivity and suffer from incomplete knowledge. So if you adopt this method, be sure to bring in the voices of defectors from rival companies as well as consultants, customers, dealers, and others who know the industry well. Make use of any survey data your market research has gathered. What you want is an unvarnished assessment of where your company is strong and weak relative to key competitors.

**TABLE 5-1**

### Rate relative strengths

|  | Company 1 | Company 2 | Company 3 | Our company |
|---|---|---|---|---|
| New-product dynamism | 8 ↓ | 4 → | 5 → | 9 → |
| Product quality | 8 ↓ | 9 → | 4 ↑ | 7 ↑ |
| Distribution | 6 → | 10 → | 6 → | 5 → |
| Customer service | 3 ↑ | 7 → | 5 ↑ | 5 → |
| Customer satisfaction | 7 ↓ | 6 → | 5 ↑ | 7 ↑ |

Strength 1–10; 10 is best

→ No change

↑ Getting better

↓ Getting worse

This assessment gives you a snapshot of the situation as it exists *at the moment.* The competitive marketplace, however, is always in flux. Your own company, for example, may be getting progressively better in terms of product quality. So it's wise to establish a trajectory for the competitive factors that matter most—thus, the arrows pointing upward, downward, or sideways in the table. By adding these trajectories, we can see that company 1, which has high overall ratings, is sliding in its competitive stance, whereas company 3 is coming up on most dimensions of competitive strength. By understanding where these competitors are headed, you'll have a better sense of the competitive situation you will confront in the months and years ahead. The current situation is less important.

### The Aggression Factor

Some companies are more aggressive than others in attacking new markets or defending their turf. You'd have to count Dell as an aggressive company. Having conquered much of the personal computer terrain among individuals, businesses, and government, it has turned its sights on the $43 billion per year printer market now dominated by Hewlett-Packard. Storage systems and servers are also in Dell's sights. As of late 2005 it remains to be seen how Hewlett-Packard will respond to Dell's threat to its lucrative printer business.

As you analyze your competitors, try to develop a systematic understanding of how they react to threats and opportunities. A matrix like the one shown in table 5-2 can help you think through and record your sense of the aggression factor. By understanding *all* these characteristics of your competitors, you can design marketing strategies that will increase your chances of coming out on top.

One way to understand how another company will respond to your actions is through role-playing. This involves studying the rival's past behavior and then assigning a team to play its part in a simulation. The military does this all the time. For example, during the cold war era, the U.S. Army's armored divisions trained in mock combat against aggressor units of soldiers schooled in the methods and doctrine of Soviet armored warfare. More recently, both armored and infantry units slated for service in Iraq were sent to a

**TABLE 5-2**

## How we and competitors react

|  | Company 1 | Company 2 | Company 3 | Our company |
|---|---|---|---|---|
| Aggressive offense | ✓ | | | |
| Aggressive defense | | | | ✓ |
| Slow in defensive response | ✓ | ✓ | ? | |
| Willing to cut prices to attack or defend | | | ✓ | ✓ |
| Will match promotions | ✓ | ✓ | ✓ | ✓ |

mock-up of a Middle Eastern city, where they engaged in war gaming against other soldiers who had adopted the methods of the Iraqi insurgency—ambushes, roadside bombs, and so forth.

Marketers can learn much from similar gaming, and a number of computer-based products are available for that purpose.

## Porter's Five Forces Framework

No discussion of the competitive environment would be complete without some discussion of Michael Porter's five forces framework. First articulated in 1979 in an award-winning *Harvard Business Review* article, "How Competitive Forces Shape Strategy," Porter's framework remains a useful tool for getting an analytical grasp on the state of competition and the underlying economics within an industry.[2] It also encourages the strategist—and the marketer—to look outside the small circle of current competing rivals to other actors and influences that determine potential profitability and growth.

Porter identified five forces that govern industry competition (see figure 5-2):

• The threat of new entrants

• The bargaining power of suppliers

• Jockeying for position among current competitors

**FIGURE 5-2**

## Porter's five forces

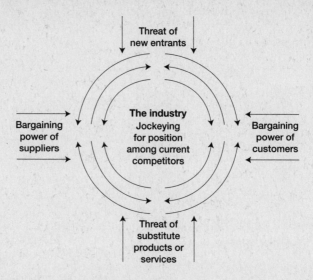

*Source:* Michael E. Porter, "How Competitive Forces Shape Strategy," *Harvard Business Review,* March–April 1979, 141. Reproduced with permission.

- The bargaining power of customers

- The threat of substitute products or services

"The collective strength of these forces," Porter writes, "determines the ultimate profit potential of an industry." Owing to these factors, the profit potential will vary from industry to industry. Today, for example, sectors of the telecommunications industry are faced with weak profit potential because many factors conspire against existing providers: industry participants are continually fighting to grab their rivals' customers, often by cutting prices and extending services; customers can switch easily; and many communications options are available, including land lines, cell phones, e-mail, instant messaging, and Internet phone service. Meanwhile, the rapid pace of technological change is forcing the existing players to spend heavily to remain on the cutting edge. Participants in other industries, in contrast, may confront a much more favorable combination of the five forces.

The key to growth and survival, according to Porter, is to use one's knowledge of these five forces to "stake out a position that is less vulnerable to attack from head-to-head opponents, whether established or new, and less vulnerable to erosion from the direction of buyers, suppliers, and substitute goods." Such a position, he argues, can be gained by solidifying relationships with profitable customers, by differentiating the product (through either redesign or marketing), by integrating operations, or by gaining technical leadership.[3]

A complete discussion of the five forces framework is beyond the scope of this book. We encourage you to obtain the article and apply its concepts to your own industry.

Failing to recognize and realistically assess competitive forces is perhaps the biggest sin that a marketer can commit. Managers who give insufficient attention to competitive analysis are usually blindsided or outflanked by rivals. Don't let this happen to you. Make a habit of studying your competitors and understanding them as well as you understand your customers. Keep your eyes open for indications of changing tactics on their part, and for the emergence of new competitors and substitutes. Test their responsiveness periodically on different fronts to see how they react: a promotional offer here, an ad blitz there.

## Summing Up

- The starting point of competitive analysis is the identification of competitors—tomorrow's as well as today's.

- Determine the strategies and objectives of your competitors.

- To better understand where key competitors are concentrating their product development and marketing efforts, create a positioning map.

- Develop a "relative strengths" table to rate the strengths and weaknesses of each competitor on key market dimensions (quality, distribution, etc.). Be sure to indicate the apparent trajectory of these market players on these dimensions.

- Determine how each key competitor reacts to moves by you and other firms. Is it slow to react? Is it aggressive in the offense? Will it fight hard to defend its turf?

## 6

# Branding

## *Differentiation That Customers Value*

## Key Topics Covered in This Chapter

- *How commodity products and services are differentiated*

- *Various approaches to differentiation*

- *Differentiating through branding*

COMMODITY STATUS IS the nightmare of every marketing manager and every salesperson. A *commodity* is a product or service for which there are no differentiating features: a liter of aviation fuel; a quart of milk; six cubic meters of cement mix; the sale of two thousand shares of IBM on the New York Stock Exchange. Once people view a product or service as a commodity, the most important thing to them is the price, and that can put sellers in a race to the bottom. To get orders, producers must meet expected standards of quality *and* have the lowest price.

Not every commodity product or service started out with that label. A flight from Boston to Washington, D.C., was once a memorable voyage. Every airline that flew that route boasted of some unique amenity. For many passengers, air travel was new and exciting. Today, that same flight is a commodity—a bus with wings—no matter which airline logo is on the rudder.

Even the personal computer, a unique and highly differentiated item when it went mainstream in the 1980s, is now approaching commodity status. More than 90 percent of current machines use the same operating systems and compatible microprocessors. For most users, any Windows machine made in the past few years is interchangeable with any other. The PC is fast on its way to joining the toaster, the refrigerator, and the television set as a commodity product. IBM's sales of its PC operation to China's Lenovo Group is only one indication of the personal computer's gradual descent from new-exciting-cool to commodity status.

Consider some of the terms we routinely use to distinguish between commodity and noncommodity goods and services.

| Commodity | Noncommodity |
|---|---|
| Widely available | Exclusive |
| Cheap and getting cheaper | Expensive |
| Standard | Unique |
| Low status | High status |
| Undifferentiated | Differentiated |

Sellers want to avoid a commodity image, because doing so usually allows them to command a higher price. Ideally, they'd like to acquire a strong *brand* status, which sets their offering apart and surrounds it with a positive aura. This chapter addresses the issues of differentiation and branding and presents ideas for using them to make your product or service stand out from the crowd.

## Differentiation of Commodity Products and Services

Companies can still make handsome fortunes with commodity and commodity-like offerings if they can differentiate their offerings on some basis. Southwest Airlines' low-fare, no-frills service has been highly profitable every year over the past three decades, even during years when its competitors were losing their shirts—and that seems to be most years. Southwest's success is based on its operating efficiency, the high utilization of its aircraft, and the productivity of its people. Together, these have made Southwest the most powerful brand in the U.S. air travel industry.

Similarly, Nucor has been highly profitable in a highly competitive, commodity industry: selling bar and rolled steel. Much of its success can be attributed to the low-cost thin-slab continuous casting process it pioneered and, like Southwest, to its innovative management of people.

Despite these exceptions, the road to profitability and growth for most enterprises is through *differentiation*, which seeks to set a company's offers apart from those of competitors in meaningful ways other than price. As you'll see later, effective differentiation is associated with the concept of branding.

A commodity producer can always differentiate on the basis of service. Although price and product features may be identical, it is still possible to differentiate on this basis. The cement business provides an example. Cement is cement, right? That's a fact that Mexico-based Cemex, the world's third-largest provider of cement, is faced with. Nevertheless, Cemex has developed a capacity for fast and reliable delivery that qualitatively differentiates its product from those of its many rivals.

As described by David Bovet and Joseph Martha in their book on supply-chain excellence, Cemex has become a major industry power in many markets because it adopted a production and high-tech logistics strategy that achieves on-time delivery 98 percent of the time, versus the 34 percent record of most competitors. For construction companies operating on tight schedules, that reliability is highly valued, especially when a late delivery means that dozens of highly paid crew members will be standing around doing nothing. "This super reliability," write Bovet and Martha, "allows [Cemex] to charge a premium in most markets, contributing to profit levels 50 percent higher than those of its key competitors."[1] In this case, super reliability has effectively differentiated a commodity product. You can achieve something similar by offering superior customer support.

Producers can also dress up their commodity products in ways that make them stand out. For example, dairy farmers in Vermont, like dairy farmers elsewhere, were faced with woefully low prices for their milk. It was a buyer's market. And milk is milk, right? Peter and Bunny Flint of Tunbridge, Vermont, changed that. In 1989 they switched to organic production, and the next year they founded Organic Cow of Vermont. Today, seventy-five certified organic dairy farmers in and around the northeastern United States supply milk to Organic Cow, which commands a price premium over regular milk in grocery stores and supermarkets.

## Approaches to Differentiation

Approaches to differentiation are limited only by the human imagination, but they generally take one of these forms:

- Appealing design—for example, Braun kitchen products

- Superior performance—for example, the Apple PowerBook, Porsche and Lexus automobiles

- Technical innovation—for example, hybrid-powered vehicles introduced by Toyota and Honda

- Reliability and durability—for example, Maytag appliances

- Convenience and ease of ordering—for example, Amazon.com

- Owner safety—for example, Volvo and Saab automobiles

A vendor can also differentiate itself through what many refer to as *atmospherics:* the physical or psychological environment in which business is conducted. This can be a powerful differentiator. Many people look for a satisfying environment in which to make their purchases, and they are willing to pay for it. Examples include Starbucks, whose Wi-Fi and café ambiance many find agreeable, and Borders bookstores, where customers can sit on a comfortable sofa and sip cappuccino as they preview their purchases.

Jordan's Furniture, a family-owned furniture retailer with five stores in the Boston area, provides customers with what can only be described as over-the-top atmospherics. Brothers Barry and Eliot Jordan and their associates don't simply provide the standard, demure room displays; they've added something unexpected. Two of their stores have IMAX theaters and restaurant facilities. One features a thrill ride, and the other has a trapeze facility in which kids, and their elders, can test their nerves and mettle above a safety net.

These stores have become more than retail outlets; they have become destinations, drawing crowds of four thousand or more shoppers on weekends. While the kids are aboard M.O.M—the Motion Odyssey Movie thrill ride that takes them on a high-speed police

chase through a mine shaft and into the alligator-infested Ever-
glades—their parents are buying furniture. Jordan's sells roughly
$950 in merchandise per square foot, versus the U.S. industry aver-
age of $150. Furthermore, its inventory turns over an eye-popping
thirteen times per year, versus one or two times for the industry.
(Virtual tours of the company's stores can be accessed through its
Web site, www.jordans.com.)

### Branding

*Branding* is another approach to differentiation. One could make a
case that branding is the culmination of efforts to differentiate product or service. By building a positive and familiar image for your offering, you have a better than even chance of becoming the buyer's
first choice among many competitors. Consider this hypothetical
but familiar example:

> *The Schmidt family was driving west on U.S. Interstate I-80 on the first
> day of their vacation. The children were sleepy. It was time to find lodg-
> ing. As they approached the next town, they began to see roadside adver-
> tisements for hotels and motels: Jim and Julia's Motel, The Iowa Lodge,
> Holiday Inn, and several others. The Schmidts exited the highway and
> drove directly to the Holiday Inn, where they checked in for the night.*

Why did this family almost reflexively select the Holiday Inn?
Most likely, they chose Holiday Inn because it was a recognizable
brand whose features and perceived benefits they valued.

A strong brand either will become the default choice when the
customer goes to make a purchase, or—the next best outcome—it
will get the product or service onto the short list of possible choices.
In our example, the Holiday Inn brand was the default choice of the
Schmidt family, given the range of options, all of which were un-
knowns. The Schmidt family knew in advance what to expect in
terms of price and quality from Holiday Inn, but knew nothing
about the others. They knew that they would experience no unhappy surprises by choosing the name brand, and this made their
choice easy.

But what would have happened if the Schmidts' list of options had included one other strong brand, such as Econo Lodge or Marriott? The Schmidts' automatic decision in favor of Holiday Inn might not have happened. They would most likely have pondered their choices.

Situations like this one encourage companies to work diligently and spend lavishly on branding their offerings. Companies also go to great lengths to defend their brands from illegal encroachment or anything else that might blur or tarnish their image. Some brands have become so successful that they have entered the American vocabulary. Thus, when President George W. Bush asked for significant reform of the Social Security system in early 2005, he said that he would not accept a Band-Aid solution. Band-Aid, an adhesive bandage, is a brand of Johnson & Johnson, one that is more than seventy-five years old. And how many times have you requested a Xerox copy of a paper document or asked, "Do you have a Kleenex?" when you were about to sneeze. For more on branding, see "Brand Vocabulary."

Whether they deserve it or not, brand-name products have an aura of quality or utility that rival products in the same category do not possess (see "The World's Top Brands"). That aura usually translates into premium prices over nonbranded rivals. Brand power also leads to higher unit sales, because customers don't have to agonize over whether or not to buy them. As Patrick Barwise and Seán Meehan have written, "Familiar brands reduce risks in a reliable, affordable, convenient way."[2] A recognizable brand acts as an imprimatur of reliability, making the consumer's choice easy. This leads to repeat sales for products like Crest toothpaste and Tide detergent, because people don't have the time or energy to compare and consider other products when they are shopping. When people find something that works for them they tend to stay with it. So they reflexively add Crest and Tide to their shopping carts.

The power of some categories of consumer packaged-goods brands may be diminishing, however, as customers come to understand that the aura of superiority may be nothing more than a curtain of advertising, and that nonbranded products may deliver the

# Brand Vocabulary

As described in *Brand New: How Entrepreneurs Earned Consumers' Trust from Wedgewood to Dell,* business historian Nancy F. Koehn defines *brand* as "a name, logo, or symbol intended to distinguish a particular seller's offering from those of competitors." It also embodies the abundant marketing messages connected with the offering and the complex set of customer expectations that arise from it.

As mentioned earlier, *branding* refers to the communication effort that aims to differentiate a product or service from its rivals and to create a positive attitude toward it. Maytag did this with a long-running ad campaign that featured the Maytag appliance repairman—"the loneliest guy in town"—sitting in his office, waiting for the phone to ring. Of course, the phone never rang because of the implied reliability of Maytag appliances.

*Brand equity,* in turn, is the financial value of a brand to a firm. For example, when Procter & Gamble acquired Gillette in early 2005, it did not pay $57 billion for Gillette's facilities, plants, and product inventory. These could have been purchased for a fraction of that princely sum. No, P&G paid that much because of the value of Gillette's consumer brands, which it saw as reliable cash generators for years to come.

One can estimate the value of brand equity by comparing the net present value of future cash flows from a branded product to the net present value of cash flows over the same number of years from an equivalent, but nonbranded, product. The difference between the two is brand equity. The calculation should include all the costs of building and supporting the brand through promotion.

*Brand extension* is the act of attaching a successful brand name to another product or service. That product or service may be weakly or strongly related to the original. For example, not many years ago, Dove, a producer of highly regarded chocolate-covered ice cream bars, created a new line of premium chocolate bars. These new bars were automatically invested with the positive aura of Dove's ice cream product. Brand extensions like this one make it less risky and less expensive to introduce new products. There is a risk, however, that extending the brand name to a mediocre new product—or to too many new products—will debase the value of the original brand.

SOURCE: Nancy F. Koehn, *Brand New* (Boston: Harvard Business School Press, 2001), 5.

same utility at significantly lower cost. This understanding is gaining ground as supermarkets and drugstores place their lower-cost generic products side-by-side with more expensive brands.

At CVS, a major U.S. drugstore chain, for example, the store's generic pain killer and fever reducer sits on the shelf next to Johnson & Johnson's Tylenol, one of the most powerful nonprescription drug

## The World's Top Brands

What are the most recognized brands? The answer depends on where you live and varies over time. In late 2004 the online magazine *Brandchannel* asked ad executives, brand managers, and academics, "Which brands had the most impact on your life in 2004?" Almost two thousand people responded. Here were their picks, ranked and ordered by geographic region:

|  | 1 | 2 | 3 | 4 | 5 |
|---|---|---|---|---|---|
| Global | Apple | Google | IKEA | Starbucks | Al Jazeera |
| Central and Latin America | Cemex | Corona | Bacardi | Bimbo | Vina Concha y Toro |
| Asia Pacific | Sony | Samsung | LG | Toyota | Lonely Planet |
| Europe and Africa | IKEA | Virgin | H&M | Nokia | Al Jazeera |
| North America | Apple | Google | Target | Starbucks | Pixar |

SOURCE: Adapted from data in Robin D. Rusch, "Readers Pick Apple: 2004 Readers Choice Award," www.brandchannel.com/features_effect.asp?pf_id=248.

brands. Both have the same active ingredient: acetaminophen. In one size and type, the CVS brand costs $8.68, whereas the Tylenol costs $15.99. The difference is enough to make a shopper think twice, and many, seeing little difference between the two, make the switch to the nonbranded house product.

## Differentiation That Matters

Is your company following a strategy of differentiation (and who isn't)? If it is, what sets your offerings apart from those of your rivals? Whatever the answer, remember this: differentiation matters only to the extent that *customers value the difference*. If the customers you've targeted truly value the difference that sets your product or service apart, they will either (1) select yours over others, (2) be willing to pay a premium for what you offer, or (3) act on some combination of 1 and 2. Experience and market research are the best ways to determine whether your difference is valued by customers.

There is growing evidence, however, that many physical products fail to differentiate themselves in ways that customers really value. Company marketers and product developers sometimes add bells and whistles to new and enhanced product versions without giving much thought about whether customers care about or are willing to pay for them. Did car buyers really ask for a choice between ten wheel covers, six types of interior upholstery, and eighteen unique steering wheels? After years of hyping these features, the Japanese carmaker that offered them figured out that few people cared.

Do consumers want the many capabilities built into their DVD players, VHS machines, digital cameras, and office software suites? Engineers love these things and dedicate enormous effort to making them part of their products. This explains why new editions of successful textbooks get longer instead of better, growing over time to the size of the New York City phone book. It explains why every new version of Microsoft Word and Excel gets bigger and more complex, even though 90 percent of users probably use only a small fraction of these capabilities.

There is an alternative to differentiation overload: being "simply better." According to Patrick Barwise and Seán Meehan, improving on the basics—what they call "generic category benefits"—will set a product or service apart. In their view, being the best at what matters to customers produces a winner, and in many cases being the best is achieved when a product or service performs as it should, is easy to buy and operate, and is backed by excellent service.

Barwise and Meehan argue that most companies have taken differentiation so far that they have left their customers behind. In the view of these authors, the emphasis on being different is probably driven by ad people, who desperately need something different to talk about so as to cut through the smog of contemporary media. In advertising today, you must say something very different—even outlandish—to be noticed. But according to these two scholars, many customers don't want bells and whistles and other differentiators as much as they want quality products, reliable service, on-time delivery, and fair value for their money. If you can deliver on these requirements better than others, you may have all the differentiation you need to be successful.

## Summing Up

- Products and services can be differentiated in many ways, including customer service, rapid delivery, appealing design, superior performance, technical innovation, convenience, safety, atmospherics, and reliability.

- A brand is distinguished not only by a name or logo but also by the marketing messages connected with the offering.

- A brand with a positive image makes the consumer's choice easy.

- Differentiation matters only to the extent that customers value the difference.

# 7

# The Right Customers

*Acquisition, Retention, and Development*

## Key Topics Covered in This Chapter

- *Understanding how customers differ in economic value*

- *Knowing where to focus customer acquisition and retention resources*

- *Identifying the sources and causes of customer defections*

- *Gaining a greater share of the wallet*

TRANSACTIONS ARE THE basis of commerce for the mass marketer, whose goal is to make a product readily available to everyone through effective distribution and low prices, and to employ advertising to entice customers to buy. Many companies, in contrast, offer products and services that involve some form of continuing relationship with customers: a credit card or bank account, a book club membership, the relationships between a parts supplier and its manufacturer customer.

These relationships give you opportunities to learn more about the people you serve and to use that greater knowledge to improve your offerings and your business. This chapter examines the underlying economics of customer relationships and offers suggestions for profitably maintaining and expanding them over time.

## Customer Economics

Not all customers are of equal economic value to a company. Eric Almquist, Andy Pierce, and César Paiva have observed huge disparities in the profitability of customers. "In our experience," they write, "many companies earn 150 percent or more of their profits from a third of their customers, break even on the middle third, and run significant losses on the bottom third."[1] What one group creates in profits is frittered away in trying to serve another. The authors note that this pattern cuts across industries. Perhaps you have observed the same in your business.

Differences in profitability are a function of several factors: total revenues, profit margins on those revenues, the duration of the customer relationship, and the cost of acquiring, serving, and retaining particular customers—good and bad. In most cases the costs are roughly the same. Consequently, substantial sums are wasted on efforts to acquire and do business with people who buy very little. The problem is compounded when marketers spend still more money trying to retain these low-value customers. They confuse loyalty with profitability. This confusion encourages them to spend money on activities aimed at retaining customers who contribute little or nothing to company profits. That's throwing good money after bad.

Conceptually, the economic value of an individual customer (or group) is the present value of the stream of cash flow generated by that individual minus the initial cost of acquiring that customer, as shown in figure 7-1. As Robert Wayland and Paul Cole describe it, "The size and value of this cash flow stream depends on the customer's volume of purchases per period, the margin on those purchases, and the duration of the relationship."[2] For example, in figure 7-1 we observe negative cash flow for a short time as the company spends money on direct mail catalogs, sales calls, or other means of acquiring customers. Cash flow in this figure eventually turns positive and increases over time as the customer does more business with the company. (For details on this concept, see "Customer Equity.")

This is the ideal picture that every marketing program should strive for. Many companies in many industries realize this cash flow pattern. For example, consider figure 7-2. This is Frederick Reichheld's representation of customer profitability in the U.S. credit card industry. Here we observe a rising stream of year-to-year profits following an initial acquisition cost. It explains why credit card companies are willing to absorb the cost of four to six months of interest-free account balances (a popular method of customer acquisition). The acquisition cost is high, but if the creditor can then retain the customer over many years, it will be amply rewarded.

**FIGURE 7-1**

**Economic value of a customer**

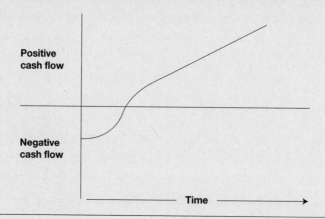

For most companies, however, reality is bound to fall short of the ideal shown in the two figures. Some of their customers linger in the negative cash flow area for a frustratingly long time before popping above breakeven. Even then, the positive cash flows they create may be anemic. Others never get out of negative territory. This underscores the disparity of economic value among customers and the importance of knowing which ones provide the greatest and least value.

## Customer Equity

Customers produce a stream of revenues—either short-term or enduring, or flat or growing with time. There is a real economic cost associated with these cash flows: the cost of acquiring, retaining, and developing (ARD) customers and their revenue streams. The difference between revenues and the cost of ARD is customer equity. Customer equity is the basis of shareholder value. When a customer defects, the stream of cash and resulting equity are lost to the firm.

Because the cost of ARD is probably similar for all customers, it makes sense for companies to be very clear about the customers they want to target and acquire.

FIGURE 7-2

**Customer life cycle profit pattern in the credit card industry**

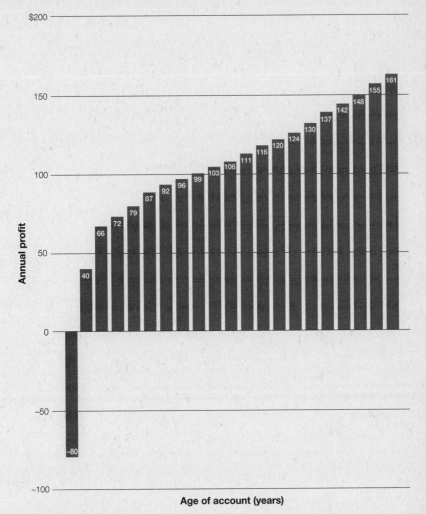

*Source:* Frederick Reichheld, *The Loyalty Effect* (Boston: Harvard Business School Press, 1996), 51. Reproduced with permission.

In the absence of steps to prevent it, a company's customer base is likely to follow a normal distribution around an average customer value, as shown in figure 7-3. In this case, the average value is arbitrarily located dead center in the bell-shaped curve, with the economically valuable customers to the right, and unprofitable ones to

FIGURE 7-3

## Customer value distribution

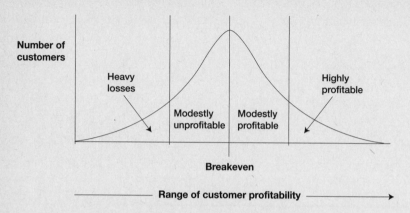

Number of
customers

Heavy
losses

Highly
profitable

Modestly
unprofitable

Modestly
profitable

Breakeven

Range of customer profitability ⟶

*Source:* Robert E. Wayland and Paul M. Cole, *Customer Connections* (Boston: Harvard Business School Press, 1997), 120. Adapted with permission.

the left. This type of distribution can be found in almost every industry, even among "nonprofit" organizations.

A museum, for example, typically loses money on every member who does nothing more than pay the annual $40 fee, receive the monthly members' magazine, and make free use of museum galleries. Organizations like these break into the money only when members pay to attend special events, shop in the gift store, eat in the café, and respond generously to periodic fund-raising drives.

A similar distribution of customer value can also be found within most targeted market segments. Doing a good job of segmenting and designing your offer for your targeted segments can skew the distribution in your favor—by putting more customers under the profitable sections of the curve. But making a profit from every customer is rare.

It's obvious in figure 7-3 that a company can improve its bottom line by doing the following.

**STOP DOING BUSINESS WITH PEOPLE WHO PERSISTENTLY GENERATE LOSSES.** Marketers and salespeople are generally optimistic. In their view, there is always a possibility that today's uneconomic account can be developed into tomorrow's profit maker. At some point, however, you must face the fact that some of these accounts will not become profitable, and they should be culled. The money you save should be redirected toward the attraction and retention of profitable accounts.

Before you cull these customers, however, it is smart to investigate the customer's situation. Does the loyal but unprofitable customer have the financial capacity to do much more business with you? If the problem is financial incapacity, drop the customer. If the problem is that you are not getting your "share of the wallet," you need to make the relationship worthwhile; something in your offer may be getting in the way—something that could be remedied.

**DEVELOP AN ECONOMICALLY SOUND PLAN FOR MOVING MODESTLY PROFITABLE CUSTOMERS INTO THE HIGH-PROFIT SECTOR.** Here's where customer knowledge pays off. Once you understand what customers want and are willing to pay for, you can create an offer they will find more attractive, perhaps by redesigning your current product or service. Consider the case of telecom giant Verizon. In mid-2005, digital subscriber line (DSL) Internet service through Verizon cost only $30 per month, perhaps enough to provide a tiny profit—as long as customers weren't spending hours talking to customer service reps about connection problems. But Verizon quickly expanded its offer to these DSL users, adding online business and computer courses, movie and music downloads, broadband-based telephone service, Web pages, and more. This offer expansion helped increase the value of many subscribers.

An alternative approach to dealing with marginally profitable customers is to work the cost side of the customer equity equation. Find less costly ways to acquire and serve these customers. Many companies are doing this via "self-service" Web sites.

**CREATE A PLAN FOR RETAINING CUSTOMERS IN THE PROFITABLE SECTORS AND DEVELOPING THEIR ECONOMIC VALUE STILL FURTHER.** These customers are the jewels in the crown. Use some of the cash saved by eliminating uneconomic customers to cement and expand your relationship with profitable ones. We treat development and retention in the balance of this chapter.

What is the value of your customers over the lifetime of their purchases, and what are your expenditures in serving them? You can estimate that value if you are willing to make assumptions about the number of lifetime transactions, the number of purchases made in each transaction, the average purchase price, and other variables on both sides of the revenue–cost ledger. The appendix contains a worksheet titled "Calculating the Lifetime Value of a Customer" that you can use for this purpose. If you go to our Web site, www.elearning.hbsp.org/businesstools, you'll find an Excel-based version that will crunch the numbers for you.

## Customer Retention

We noted earlier that every profitable customer who defects deprives you of a cash flow stream that might otherwise have continued for many years. That hurts the bottom line. Worse, replacing a lost customer requires additional investments in marketing and purchase inducements, such as rebates and discounts. These acquisition expenditures may offset revenues from customer purchases for a year or more. Retention is particularly important when the costs of acquisition are high.

By some measures, even a modest improvement in customer retention can substantially improve the bottom line. For example, a study by Frederick Reichheld and W. Earl Sasser Jr. of companies in nine industries—from auto service to software—found that a 5 percent reduction in the rate of customer defection boosted profits by 25 to 85 percent.[3] Those are huge profit improvements!

Given the economic value of retention, it is surprising that companies don't give more formal and systematic attention to it. They spend heavily on activities that aim to acquire new customers and squeeze sales out of existing ones. They manage these activities intensely. They have advertising managers, sales managers, sales quotas, and even prizes for the people who open the most new accounts. Far less attention is given to the systematic management of customer retention, even though, if Reichheld and Sasser are correct, a dollar invested on the latter will pay higher dividends than a dollar spent on the former. Just be sure that you focus retention spending on customers who provide positive economic value, and not on the profitless bottom tier.

## Quantify Defection

What is the pattern of customer defection for your enterprise? Do you know the rate and reasons for defection? Do you know the average revenue loss resulting from each defection? If you cannot answer these questions, you are missing a huge part of customer knowledge—and customer knowledge is the foundation of successful marketing.

The first job of retention management is to estimate the rate of customer defection, or turnover. If you don't have the information in your database, follow this method, as recommended by Frederick Reichheld. Count the number of customer defections over a period of months; then annualize that number. For example, if you had 100 defections in one quarter (three months), the annual rate would be 400 defections. Supposing that you have 2,000 accounts, that's one-fifth, or a 20 percent annual defection rate. Turn the 1/5 fraction on its head, and you have 5/1, or 5, the number of years that you can expect the average customer to stay with you, given the current defection rate.[4] Assuming that you can also determine the average annual customer contribution to profits, you can use this number to calculate the present value of the average customer.

## Locate the Epicenter of Defection

If your business is like most, it markets several product lines to different segments. That being the case, it's likely that you'll have different rates of defection within these sectors. This provides a case for quantifying defection (using the method just described) within each area.

You may find, for example, that customer turnover among subscribers to your online stock research service is 50 percent but that the rate is only 10 percent among your bond market data service. This understanding will help you focus your efforts to tame customer turnover.

Further analysis may give you insights into the characteristics of defecting customers. For example, analysis may indicate that within the stock research service, males between twenty-five and thirty-five years of age account for 90 percent of defections. Armed with that information, you might decide, owing to the high cost of customer acquisition, to target older customers.

### Learn from Defectors and the Dissatisfied

Defecting customers are a critical source of information. If you can contact them and get them to respond, they can tell you things about your offer that encouraged their defection.

> "I didn't feel that the advice in your stock market newsletter was worth the price."

> "The magazine is too long on ads and too short on content."

> "We didn't renew our season tickets because the symphony is performing too many modern pieces. We prefer baroque."

> "My child had two ineffective teachers last year, and the administration did nothing to improve the situation. We won't pay private school tuition for that type of performance."

> "Your home delivery grocery service was fine, and the prices were competitive. We stopped using the service because we've gone to a nontraditional diet of organic foods."

Remarks like these can help you understand the cause of customer defections and guide you in making choices about pricing, product or service features, delivery, and other aspects of your offer. So develop a systematic approach to obtaining feedback from defectors.

### Neutralize the Causes of Defection

Assuming that your value proposition is attractive and on target (you sell a needed product or service, it is priced right, and it is delivered right), the best way to minimize defection is to eliminate reasons for customers to look elsewhere. Here are specific guidelines:

- **Do not disappoint.** Product or service quality must be consistent and must be maintained at the high level people have come to expect.

- **Keep the price reasonable.** Milking customers may provide a short-term benefit, but it will encourage defection.

- **Maintain a dialogue with customers.** Customers will forgive one or two lapses if they have opportunities to provide feedback. Reward that feedback in some way.

- **Keep looking for ways to surprise and delight customers.** If people anticipate five-day delivery, improve your fulfillment process to the point that you can deliver in four days. Then look for opportunities to surprise and delight on some other front.

## Customer Development

Once you've established a customer-vendor relationship, front-end acquisition costs are behind you. If you've done a good job of retention, you'll lose some customers, but you will not have to start over again with a new cast. The next challenge is to expand the amount of profitable business you can conduct with current customers. Many refer to this activity as *customer development*, or as expanding your share of the wallet.

In figure 7-2, you saw how credit card customers are a source of increasing profits as the years go by. Why is that? Chances are that the average credit card customer uses his card more often as he becomes accustomed to it. He may be running up balances that are not paid off every month—another component of revenue for the card company. If he owns a small business, he may acquire another card account and use it for travel costs and for sizable purchases of business supplies and equipment. Cross-selling creates still more opportunities to develop this customer's transaction base. The MBNA cardholder, for example, may decide to invest in a certificate of deposit, start a retirement account, finance a car purchase, or take out a home equity loan. MBNA makes these and other financial services available to cardholders in its effort to capture a larger share of the wallet.

Each of the activities just described is a form of customer development. Assuming that a customer is satisfied with your current products and service, it is often easier to expand your business with that customer than to identify and acquire a new one. This is why customer development is an important part of customer relationship management. What are you doing to develop the customer accounts you now have?

Customer development requires that you find new ways to address customer needs. Conceptually, one of the best ways to begin is to understand the customer's value chain. A value chain is a set of related activities that turns inputs into outputs. For example, the household that does its own dirty laundry has a chain of activities that includes the following, as shown in figure 7-4: purchasing and operating washing and drying machines, buying detergent, providing a supply of water, and providing periodic maintenance of the machines.

Typically, a manufacturer sells its washers and dryers through a retailer. The customer then turns to others for all other parts of the chain: to a supermarket for detergent, to the local municipality for water, and to a local appliance repair shop for maintenance. If the manufacturer wanted to expand its share of the wallets of its retail purchasers, it could sell detergent "specially formulated for your machine" by direct mail, or sell annual maintenance and repair con-

**FIGURE 7-4**

**The clothes cleaning value chain**

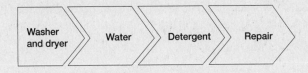

tracts. Obviously, this company must target only those links in the customer value chain for which it can develop a profitable and competitive advantage over those currently servicing these links.

As an exercise, sketch out the typical value chain for your current customers. Circle the link or links you are now serving through your marketing and product development programs. Next, identify other links that you might feasibly address in the future. Then ask these questions:

- What customer information would you need to have before addressing these new parts of the value chain?

- How are customers currently handling those links, and through whom? Are they satisfied, or are they open to alternatives?

- Do we currently have the competencies to serve those links? If not, would acquiring them be feasible and worth the cost?

Granted, this is a simple approach to a complex challenge. But big things usually begin with a handful of simple questions.

As a rule, unlocking the revenue potential of existing customers is more productive and less uncertain than the expensive chore of acquiring new ones. USAA, a financial services company that caters exclusively to members of the U.S. armed forces, discovered this years ago. Over time, USAA has expanded its offerings to member-customers from auto insurance to dozens of other products: life insurance, credit cards, checking and savings accounts, and so forth. Each new service addressed one of the links in the financial value chain of its customers. Costco, a U.S. superstore, has done the same thing. Costco members can take care of more than their food and liquor needs when they visit a Costco store; they can now fill drug prescriptions, get eye examinations, purchase eyeglasses or contact lenses, and book their vacation trips through the in-house travel agent. In both examples, the vendors have expanded their share of the wallet.

## Summing Up

- Many companies experience large disparities in the economic value of various customers. They reap substantial profits from some but waste substantial sums attempting to acquire and serve others.

- Because of the cost of acquiring, retaining, and developing customers, you should be very clear about which customers you want to serve.

- Retention expenditures should be shifted from low-value customers to those who bring high profits and those who can be developed into the high-profit group.

- Even a modest improvement in customer retention can substantially improve the bottom line in some cases.

- Information obtained from defectors can help you improve pricing, product or service features, and other aspects of your offer that will help reduce customer defections.

- The best way to minimize defections is to eliminate reasons for customers to look elsewhere.

- Customer development aims to expand the amount of profitable business conducted with existing customers. One approach is to examine the customer's value chain of activities and determine which links in the chain you can profitably serve.

# 8

# Developing New Products and Services

## The Marketer's Role

## Key Topics Covered in This Chapter

- *Breakthrough and incremental new products and services*

- *Horizontal and vertical extensions of your product line*

- *The new-product process*

- *Using a stage-gate system for go–no go decisions*

- *The marketer's role in developing new products and services*

N EW PRODUCTS ARE an important element in organizational growth and survival. Faced with intense competition, changing customer expectations, and technological advances, a company must roll out the kinds of new products—and improved versions of existing ones—that keep the cash registers ringing. The decline phase of the product life cycle (described in chapter 1) underscores the importance of continually reinvigorating the revenue stream. And what is true of new products is equally true of services.

We are accustomed to thinking of new products as physical objects—electronic devices, computer software, automobiles, the latest pharmaceuticals. But new services are equally important in our economy. Consulting, mutual funds, online college courses, credit cards, home grocery delivery, and life-saving angioplasty procedures are all examples of services that provide value for customers and revenues for companies. Because the processes used to develop new services are like those used to develop products, we'll refer solely to new "products" and not "products and services" beyond this point.

New-product development is one of the business world's riskier activities. However, when it is based on a foundation of good marketing—understanding customers, market segmentation, customer targeting, and so forth—the risk can be reduced. Developing new products, and *then* figuring out how to market them, usually leads to disaster.

There are exceptions. Alexander Bell never mapped out the market for telephones, and he didn't conduct focus groups. What he knew was that telephones would be a boon to anyone who wanted to communicate over distance. In Bell's case, Ralph Waldo Emerson's quip proved true: invent a better mousetrap and the world will beat a path to your door. But the telephone was a "new to the world" innovation for which there was no comparable substitute. Most new products today, in contrast, must compete against similar products or effective substitutes. And they must clamor for the attention of consumers who are inundated by products and marketing messages.

This chapter examines the new-product development process and the role marketers must play in it. That role is large and often critical. As the primary link between the company and the world of customers and competitors, marketers are ideally placed to identify latent and unmet needs and to communicate them to their colleagues. They also lead the many activities that eventually bring a new product to market: pricing, establishing distribution channels, creating promotion plans—all the things on which a successful product launch depends.

## The Two Types of New Products

It's difficult to understand product development and the marketer's role without first understanding the various types of new products. New-product projects fall somewhere along a continuum, with breakthrough products on one extreme and incrementally altered or improved products on the other, as shown in figure 8-1. As you'll see, the opinions and inputs of customers generally have the least value for the former, and the greatest value for the latter.

### Breakthrough Products

A *breakthrough product* brings one or more of the following attributes to the market:

- An entirely new set of performance features

- Improvements in performance features that are many times greater than those found in the market

- A sizable reduction in cost for the same features offered by other products

**FIGURE 8-1**

## Breakthrough versus incremental product development

| Breakthrough ⟺ Incremental | |
|---|---|
| • New-to-the-world performance features<br>• Huge advance in performance<br>• Dramatic cost reduction | • Improvement in existing product<br>• Derivative of existing product platform<br>• Exploits existing forms or technology |
| • High risk | • Lower risk |
| • Infrequently occurring | • More frequent |
| • Costly to do | • Less costly |
| • Targeted to new or existing markets | • Targeted to existing or adjacent markets |
| **Marketing's key responsibilities** | |
| • Envision the market<br>• Create demand<br>• Educate the market | • Listen to the existing market<br>• Accommodate current demand |

These breakthrough products change the basis of competition in their industries. Examples of breakthrough products (when they were introduced) include the following:

- Electric lighting

- Antibiotics

- The jet aircraft engine

- The microwave oven

- The credit card

- The transistor

- The heart pacemaker

- Hip and knee replacements

- GPS devices

- Medical procedures that eliminate the need for invasive surgery and long hospital stays

Marketing's involvement with breakthrough products should be more general than specific in the early phases of their development. Researchers like to ask customers what they want, but because most people's frame of reference is only the world of existing products, they inevitably describe what they want in terms of what they already have. Few can imagine something entirely new—that is, something beyond their experience and understanding of technical possibilities.

So how can marketers understand what will sell? Anthony Ulwick, an innovation management consultant and author, has recommended that researchers ask potential customers about the outcomes that would please them. Ulwick cites the case of Cordis, a manufacturer of medical products. Its people asked cardiologists, surgeons, and nurses about the outcomes they sought from angioplasty procedures conducted on patients with blocked arteries—*not* the product features that would make those outcomes possible. Once the company understood the desired outcomes, Cordis's technical people turned their experience and imaginations to developing a medical device that would produce those outcomes.[1]

### Incremental Products

Incremental development projects aim for something less ambitious. They generally exploit existing forms or technologies. They either improve upon something that already exists or reconfigure an existing form or technology to serve another purpose. In this sense an *incremental product* represents innovation at the margins.

For example, Intel's Pentium IV computer chip represented an incremental improvement over its immediate predecessor, the Pentium III, because the two chips shared the same fundamental technology.

The Pentium IV incorporated design improvements that enhanced chip performance, but it didn't reinvent the wheel. Similarly, new versions of the word-processing and spreadsheet software we all use are incremental in nature. They add bells and whistles and clean up some problems, but these programs are cut from the same cloth as their predecessors; they are not radical departures. (For another angle on this, see "Cannibalization Issues.")

When compared with breakthrough products, incremental products take less time and money to develop because the core of the product remains the same; only a few features are altered to improve performance or otherwise make it more appealing to customers. When an automaker releases next year's model of its passenger cars, for example, it adds or improves a number of features at the margins while retaining the core elements of the vehicle. Visitors to the auto showroom will likely see digital dashboard features instead of analog versions. A GPS locator system may be a new option, along with improved climate control and next-generation fuel injectors. For the automaker, this "new and improved" product strategy is much less costly and time-consuming than building a new model from scratch, something that costs at least $1 billion and takes three to five years. It is also less risky because the incremental product addresses the same market, which the automaker presumably understands.

Marketers play a traditional role in the development of incremental products because customers have a frame of reference for describing what they want. Thus, more traditional research techniques (e.g., surveys and focus groups) are very helpful.

At this point you may find it useful to think about the course of product development in your own industry. Looking back over the past ten years or so, can you identify the products that really changed the basis of competition? Which would you describe as breakthroughs, and which were clearly incremental? Now look to the present:

- Are you aware of any breakthrough products in the works that will affect your industry?

- If and when those products enter the marketplace, how will they affect competition?

- How might these innovations impact your own company's sales and profitability?

## Extending Product Lines into New Segments

Marketers are always eager to extend their product lines. Once they have a successful brand, they are tempted to create derivative (incremental) products that address the needs or tastes of adjacent market segments. The power of the brand name reduces the risk of these product-line extensions (although at the risk of devaluing the brand itself).

### Cannibalization Issues

In many cases—both breakthrough and incremental—commercialization of an idea will cannibalize some part of the developer's existing business. For example, Toyota's hybrid-power vehicle, the Prius, has attracted a number of buyers who have a strong interest in the environment or fuel economy (or both). Based on positive auto reviews and feedback from owners, sales of the Prius are likely to grow in the years ahead. But we can assume that some number of these sales will be made to individuals who would have purchased other Toyota models had the innovative hybrid car not been available. Thus, the Prius will cannibalize some number of existing sales.

Product developers and managers must confront the cannibalization issue as they assess the value of their new technologies and products. In most cases they will conclude that the wisest course is to move forward with their new-product ideas and accept the fact of cannibalization. If they don't, competitors will.

Marketers generally refer to product-line extensions as either horizontal or vertical. *Horizontal* line extensions seek to appeal to different customer tastes (e.g., Coke, Diet Coke, Diet Coke with Lemon). *Vertical* lines aim to offer a product for every pocketbook or for different levels of need (e.g., Microsoft Office Home Edition and Microsoft Office Professional Edition). The "good," "better," and "best" varieties once offered by Sears, Roebuck and Co. are another example of vertical extensions. Some companies have both horizontal and vertical extensions. In almost all cases, the extensions are based on incremental development.

Alfred Sloan's General Motors was one of the most notable practitioners of the product-line concept. Under Sloan's leadership, GM mapped out a product line that aimed to satisfy buyers in every economic stage of life, with the Chevrolet brand at the bottom—for the first-time buyer of modest means—and moving progressively upscale with Pontiac, Buick, Oldsmobile, and Cadillac. The idea was that buyers would trade up to fancier and more expensive GM brands as they became more affluent. This was a vertical form of product line. But each GM division also extended its brand horizontally with, for example, the Chevrolet division producing the Impala, Corvette, Malibu, and so forth. Today, the Chevrolet line includes trucks, vans, and sport utility vehicles.

More recently, Apple has begun to extend its successful iPod digital player both vertically and horizontally, as shown in figure 8-2. These product-line extensions will probably increase as the company attempts to stake out control of meaningful segments with unique products before rivals Sony, Samsung, Dell, and others can gain traction.

The secret to profitable product-line extension, both vertically and horizontally, is the product platform. A *product platform* is described by Marc Meyer and Alvin Lehnerd, whose work has largely defined this important concept as "a set of subsystems and interfaces that form a common structure from which a stream of derivative products can be efficiently developed and produced."[2] A robust platform gives a company an enormous opportunity to develop derivative products for specific market segments at a reasonable cost.

FIGURE 8-2

**Apple's iPod line, as of April 2005**

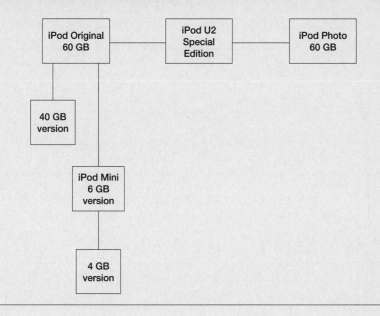

---

The ubiquitous Swatch watch is an example of a successful product family based on a common platform. The Swatch platform is a small set of timepiece subsystems linked through a few electronic interfaces. Almost every Swatch uses the same platform, which is simple, inexpensive to manufacture, and capable of supporting endless external variations.

Product platforms based on design elegance and manufacturability give companies low-cost opportunities to customize their products for different market segments, as shown in figure 8-3. In this figure you see how the platform of common elements can be joined with some unique elements to create a product (or service) for a particular market segment.

Black & Decker did this in the early 1970s. In a classic case of platform innovation, Black & Decker created a platform of electric motor and controls on which it based dozens of consumer power

**FIGURE 8-3**

## Addressing many market segments with a common platform

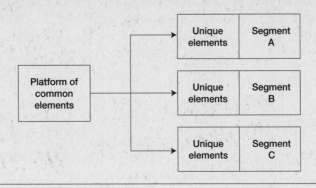

tools: electric drills, sanders, saws, grinders, and others. Thanks to that common platform and the cost advantage it conferred, Black & Decker gained leadership in many consumer power tool segments. At the same time it reduced complexity in its operations. Instead of having to manufacture and stock unique motors, components, and switches for each of its many power tools, the company accomplished its goals using a single assembly program and common set of components. Costs and components were reduced by orders of magnitude.[3] Lower costs made it possible to underprice Asian competitors and increase demand for the Black & Decker product line.

The Swatch and Black & Decker examples underscore how product developers and marketers can collaborate. When marketers discover an unexploited segment that has sales potential, they can work with developers to quickly spin out a product that appeals to customers in that segment. In each case the platform is the same; only the outer trappings of the product are different.

## The New–Product Process

Whether the new offering is of the breakthrough or incremental type, whether it is a product or a service, experienced companies use

a well-defined and time-tested process for making go–no go decisions. That process usually begins with two creative acts: idea generation and opportunity recognition (see figure 8-4).

First, a person develops an insight about something new. Idea
generation sometimes takes the form of a technical insight with no
apparent commercial application. In other cases, a customer problem
inspires the insight. Alert salespeople, service technicians, market researchers, and other company personnel often spot these problems
and turn them into profitable ventures. For example, in the 1920s, a
young 3M laboratory researcher named Dick Drew visited an auto
body repair shop in St. Paul, Minnesota, near the company's headquarters. 3M made and sold sandpaper, and Drew had gone to this
shop to test a new batch. As he entered, workers were standing
around an automobile, cursing a blue streak. The problem was a
botched paint job. To deal with the two-tone cars popular at that
time, auto body workers had to apply one color at a time, masking
the other surfaces with butcher paper, which they held in place with
a heavy adhesive tape. In this case—and apparently many others—
peeling off the tape also peeled away part of the new paint, resulting
in many hours of needed rework.

**FIGURE 8-4**

**Creating a new product**

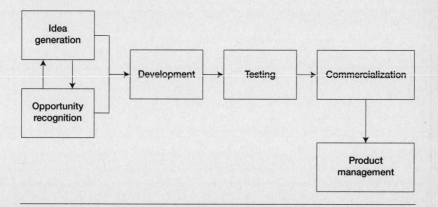

Drew might have said, "That's too bad," and gone about his business—testing his new batch of sandpaper. Instead he observed his customers' problem and perceived the need for a tape with a less powerful adhesive—one that would keep the butcher paper in place and then peel off without taking the paint with it. Drew returned to his laboratory and began a long search for materials and a manufacturing process that would solve the peeling paint problem he had observed—and others like it. After two years of experimenting with papers and adhesive formulas, Drew's persistent quest resulted in a successful new product: masking tape. That product has generated revenues for 3M for more than seven decades. More important, it spawned 3M's adhesive tape business, which produces more than seven hundred specialized products for medical, electrical, home, and industrial applications.

Opportunity recognition follows idea generation. It occurs when someone says one of three things:

1. "This idea might be of value to customers."

2. "If we could solve this problem, we could create value for our customers and our shareholders."

3. "This might produce a huge cost advantage."

Once an opportunity is recognized, it must be incubated to the point where it can be evaluated by decision makers, who need answers to several questions:

Will the idea work?

Do we have the technical know-how to make it work?

Does the idea represent value for customers?

Does the idea fit with our strategy?

Does it make sense from a cost perspective?

Ideas that produce affirmative answers to these questions and obtain organizational support are moved into some form of idea development, and then they proceed down a long and bumpy road toward technical and market testing and eventually commercialization. Commercialization is the final test. Here, customers make the final evaluation. Once a new product has established itself (and the majority do not), there is a final activity: product management over the product's life cycle.

Few of the ideas that enter this process complete the challenging journey to the marketplace. A study by Booz Allen Hamilton found that half to two-thirds of proposed products fail to complete the journey to commerialization.[4] Experienced product-generating companies accept the need to cull weak and inappropriate ideas. They know that to do otherwise would rob their few truly great ideas of the resources they need to be successful.

Every company must have a method for sorting good ideas from bad ones and to pace the development process. For many companies that method is the *stage-gate system*, which was developed by Robert Cooper in the late 1980s.[5] It features an alternating series of development stages and assessment "gates" that aims for early elimination of weak ideas and faster time to market for potential winners. These stages and gates control events from the initial idea all the way to commercialization. Figure 8-5 is a generic representation of that system. Here's how it works:

- **Stages.** Stages are phases of the process in which development work is done. For example, a system would have stages for developing the raw idea, writing the technical specifications, building a prototype, and so forth. Commercialization is the final stage.

- **Gates.** Gates are checkpoints where people with decision-making authority determine whether the project should be (1) killed, (2) sent back for more development, or (3) advanced to the next stage. Gates can be used at various points to determine strategic fit, whether the project passes technical and financial hurdles, whether it's ready for testing or launch, and so forth.

**FIGURE 8-5**

**A stage-gate system**

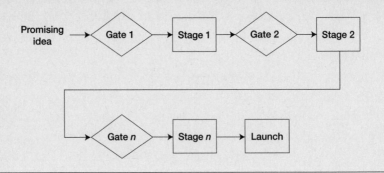

A system like this is certainly an improvement over one that is either ad hoc or arbitrary. And for product developers it is superior to a system in which they must play politics and curry favor with powerful executives to keep their projects alive and moving forward. It is also better for companies, because, if managed properly, it prevents projects of dubious value from hanging on and soaking up scarce resources that could be applied to projects having greater commercial promise.

The effectiveness of a stage-gate system, however, is no better than the decision-making teams that control each gate. These teams should

- Be experienced with innovation and product development

- Have expertise in the discipline required at their particular gate (e.g., marketing or financial analysis)

- Have the authority to extend or withdraw funding

- Be very clear about company strategy

- Be objective and unencumbered by political pressure

You can probably imagine how having the wrong decision makers at various gates could undermine the system. The wrong people are those who lack expertise or experience, are there to exert political pressure, or are out of touch with company strategy. Keep these people off your decision teams.

## The Marketer's Role

There is a clear and important role for marketing at each phase of the product development process, and at many points in the stage-gate system. These are summarized in table 8-1. In many cases, a salesperson chances upon an appealing idea, or a market researcher conducting a focus group perceives a new opportunity. In other cases, product ideas and opportunities are recognized by customers, particularly by lead users. And after an idea is generated, its opportunity must be measured—yet another point at which marketers have something to contribute.

As new ideas enter the development phase, the company will turn to marketing people for answers to critical questions at various decision gates:

- What is the market size for the proposed product, and in which customer segments can we expect the greatest acceptance?

- Are we capable of reaching these segments through existing channels of distribution? What will it cost to do so?

- What customer requirements must be satisfied, and how rapidly are those requirements changing?

- What price range will be acceptable to the market?

- Against whom will we compete?

- How would we articulate the value proposition of this new product to our customers?

The answers to most of these questions go into the business analysis and revenue-cost projections that management considers as the project approaches individual stages.

**TABLE 8-1**

## Marketing's involvement in product development

| Action | Description |
| --- | --- |
| Preliminary market assessment | This quick-and-dirty analysis takes place before a product idea enters development. It answers the question, "Should we go forward a step or two with this idea?" |
| Formal market study | Formal market research is applied before substantial development funds are allocated. |
| Field testing of prototypes | Marketing and technical personnel participate. |
| Test marketing | In some cases, particularly for packaged consumer goods, marketers use this approach to determine market acceptance of the product and its price. |
| Commercialization | Product launch is based on a formal and complete market plan for the product. |

### Early Market Exposure

As a product nears the end of development, marketers go into overdrive, this time seeking feedback from potential customers. Although much internal testing of a prototype goes on within the company—mostly geared toward performance and functionality—marketers often expose the prototype to a confidential circle of outsiders. Their judgments and recommendations will (1) inform the next go–no go decision and (2) suggest alterations or improvements that will make the final product more acceptable to its intended market. Some potential customers may be asked to use the product and give feedback, a process called beta testing.

A remarkable and imaginative instance of prototype testing was conducted by General Motors on its all-electric passenger vehicle, the Impact. Although the Impact never gained market acceptance, the method used to test it was as imaginative as it was thorough, and it gave GM engineers valuable insights into consumer attitudes and desired specifications.

As described by then GM executive Vincent Barabba in *Meeting of the Minds*, the product test had two phases: one internal and one external. In the external phase, the company produced more than one hundred prototype vehicles and, using newspaper ads, invited people in twelve U.S. cities to drive them. The GM offer was straightforward: it was looking for people to use the Impact for routine driving for a two-week period. During and after that test period, drivers would report their comments and suggestions to GM project engineers and marketers. But GM wasn't simply looking for licensed drivers—it wanted the "right" drivers, people Barabba described as innovative types, opinion leaders, market mavens, and others who had a passion for automobiles.

> *Public announcement of the study in each of the twelve cities resulted in a flood of calls to an 800 number. In Los Angeles alone, thousands of calls came in within just a few days. More than six thousand of these L.A. callers were sent a questionnaire designed to identify those few individuals who ranked high on GM's measure of innovators, opinion leaders, and market mavens. They were the people GM wanted to listen to . . . More than one-hundred respondents fit the bill as the "right people."* [6]

Each of these individuals was given the free use of an Impact electric vehicle and, as described by Barabba, were enthusiastic about helping in the further design and development of the electric auto concept. The project's chief engineer was on hand as Barabba and his market team debriefed each driver, gaining "a goldmine of informed feedback" on the prototype vehicle and many ideas for customer-pleasing improvements. Better still, the chief engineer received feedback that was unfiltered by staff information handlers.

The GM experience underscores three important tips for prelaunch product testing:

1. Prototype testing by potential users is an important method for involving customers in product development.

2. Have your prototype tested by the right people—people whose backgrounds and interests are likely to provide the greatest and most valuable insights.

3. Have the right people listen to prototype testers. By connecting key marketing and development personnel with testers, you will eliminate the chance of critical insights being lost in a morass of aggregated questionnaire data.

## Market Launch

Product commercialization (launch) is usually marketing's phase of greatest involvement with new products, particularly for breakthrough products. Marketing takes a leading role in this phase. In some cases, it will attempt to sell the product in a specific location to gauge customer acceptance and to observe how people respond to price and promotion. For example, a fast food restaurant chain might launch a new menu item in its Dallas area outlets months before the item is rolled out to the nation as a whole.

Commercialization, which begins many months before the product's actual introduction, is based on a fully developed marketing plan in which all elements of the marketing mix—product, price, distribution, and promotion—are specified and supported with budgeted resources.

## Your New–Product Strategy

What is your company's approach to developing new products (and services)? Is it ad hoc, or is it based on a well-defined process and a deliberate strategy for building growth and profits? Are your new products of the breakthrough type, or are they incremental? In developing new products, is the company a leader, a fast follower, or a laggard?

These are important questions because they involve your company's future. Because of the product life cycle of rapid growth, maturity, and decline, it is nearly impossible for a company to increase revenues (in real terms) without regular releases of new products, as shown in figure 8-6. Periodic product releases add sales volume to offset declines among older products.

## Beyond New

There is no denying the importance of new-product development. The pace of change and technological progress makes it imperative

FIGURE 8-6

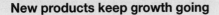

**New products keep growth going**

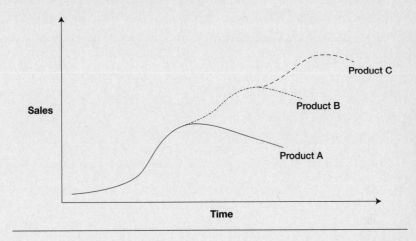

that companies develop new and better solutions to customer problems. If they don't, their rivals will.

This is not an excuse, however, for executives to take their eyes off the ball already in play. It is expensive to develop and launch new products, and few of them gain traction. Existing products, in contrast, have found their places in the market, and the substantial costs of getting them there are now history. Thus, it makes sense to continually improve the offer made by your established products to customers. Doing so can delay or moderate the natural decline of revenues that most existing products eventually experience. As Patrick Barwise and Seán Meehan write in *Simply Better,* "Innovation for innovation's sake is nonsense, but relentless innovation to improve performance on the generic category benefits is an essential element of sustained business success."[7]

Once people become comfortable and satisfied with a type of photo film, shopping in a particular supermarket, or driving a particular brand of automobile, they are not eager to jump to something else. Busy people do not make unnecessary changes if they are satisfied and comfortable with what they have; doing so disturbs their comfort, takes time, and involves risks. You can maintain their sense of comfort and satisfaction by continually improving your offer:

- Pass along part of your cost savings as price reductions.

- Upgrade product quality regularly.

- Train customer-facing employees to deliver the best possible service.

- Surprise and delight customers with samples when they don't expect them.

Every time you do this, you give customers something nice—something they hadn't anticipated. There are countless ways to improve your customers' experience that do not involve creating a new product or service. Regular improvements will make your product or service "simply better" and will keep customers in your camp *if* you focus on the things that truly matter to them.

Take a moment to think about your customers. What matters to them? What could you do this week—and every week thereafter—to improve the things that matter?

This chapter addresses many key aspects of the new-product process and looks at marketing's role in its phases. These are big issues, considering their importance in contemporary business, and we have only scratched the surface here. If you'd like to learn more, see "For Further Reading."

## Summing Up

- New products or services are either breakthrough or incremental.

- Breakthrough products change the basis of competition in their industries.

- Because most people's frame of reference is existing products, interviewees tell market researchers what they want in terms of what they already have. Few can imagine something entirely new. Consequently, researchers should try to understand the outcomes customers would value.

- Incremental products exploit existing forms or technologies. It takes less time and money to develop these products, and they present less market risk.

- Traditional market research techniques are applicable to incremental product development.

- Horizontal product-line extensions seek to appeal to different customer tastes (e.g., Hershey's Chocolate Kisses versus Chocolate Kisses with Almonds).

- Vertical product-line extensions aim to offer a product for every pocketbook or for different levels of need (e.g., good, better, best versions of the same product).

- Product platforms facilitate low-cost, incremental product-line extensions.

- The new-product development process includes idea generation, opportunity recognition, development, testing, commercialization, and product management.

- Many companies use the stage-gate system to eliminate weak product ideas and move strong ones through the development process.

- Marketers provide ideas and feedback at all gates in the stage-gate system. They go into high gear as the product approaches and enters the commercialization phase.

- New-product development is risky and expensive, but it is necessary to offset revenue losses from existing products during the decline phase of a product's life cycle. Companies can slow down or delay those losses by continuously improving their current offers to customers.

# 9

# Pricing It Right

*Strategies, Applications, and Pitfalls*

## Key Topics Covered in This Chapter

- *Pricing strategies and business objectives*

- *Cost-plus pricing*

- *Skimming and penetration pricing*

- *Pricing and the experience curve*

- *Pricing for snob appeal*

- *Stealth price increases*

- *Three uses of price promotions*

- *Pricing and customer-perceived value*

- *Pricing throughout the product life cycle*

**P**RICE IS ONE of the "four P's"—along with product, place (i.e., distribution), and promotion—of the marketing mix. And as with each of its siblings, getting the price right contributes mightily to business success or failure. Too high a price reduces unit demand, allowing competitors to take away customers; too low a price encourages more unit sales but reduces the profit margin on each sale. But what price is "too high"? Too low? Just right? The answers are determined largely by the motivations of those who set the prices and by what the market will bear.

Sellers are motivated by one or more objectives when they adopt a pricing strategy. Here are a few of the more common objectives:

- **To maximize profits.** This goal may apply in either the long run or the short run. It does not necessary translate into high prices.

- **To maximize unit sales.** This is a concern of manufacturers that need to keep their production facilities operating near capacity.

- **To gain a commanding market share.** This end, in turn, produces several strategic benefits.

- **To discourage market entry by competitors.** Prices that produce only modest profits will often discourage the entry of competitors.

- **To create a perception of brand quality or exclusiveness.** Some people think that low-priced products are cheap goods and that high-priced ones are always the best.

- **To create store traffic by slashing the price of a staple item.** This "loss leader" strategy brings people through the door.

- **To encourage trial purchases.** This approach can boost newly introduced products and services.

This chapter examines several price strategies, along with their advantages and disadvantages: cost-plus pricing; price skimming; penetration pricing; prestige pricing; bait and hook pricing; price promotions; and pricing based on customer-perceived value. No matter which approach you adopt, it should address the objectives of your marketing plan. We'll also briefly revisit the product life cycle in terms of pricing decisions.

## Cost–Plus Pricing

In a noncompetitive market, a company can get away with a cost-plus approach to pricing—that is, adding an amount or percentage to the per-unit cost of making and distributing the product. This form of pricing is often seen in government defense contracts. In cost-plus pricing, the firm guarantees itself some level of profit.

In this approach, the product's price is determined as follows:

Price = (Unit variable cost + Unit allocation to fixed costs) ×
(1 + percent markup)

Consider this example:

*Gizmo Guidance Systems has a contract to supply the Royal Air Force with advanced aircraft navigational equipment. Under the contract terms, the price of each navigational unit is determined as follows.*

*The variable cost of producing each unit (labor, components, electricity, etc.) is calculated. Gizmo's cost accountants then allocate some portion of total fixed costs (salaries, insurance, R&D, building heat, debt service, maintenance, etc.) to each of the navigational units produced under the contract. Together, these represent the full cost of producing each unit. The contract guarantees a 15 percent profit on top of these costs. For illustration, let's use these numbers:*

*Unit variable cost = $10,000*

*Unit allocation to fixed cost = $8,000*

*Profit = 15 percent*

*Unit price = ($10,000 + $8,000) × (1 + 0.15) = $20,700*

In sophisticated applications, companies use activity-based pricing, which carefully tracks all costs and overhead allocations.

Few companies are in a position to apply cost-plus pricing. In free markets, most prices are determined through competition among sellers. In these markets, cost-plus is a relic of a bygone time, when producers could push products onto the market as fast as they could make them. But those days are mostly gone forever. An innovator may establish a monopoly, but such monopolies are short-term.

Target return pricing is another technique that attempts to specify the profit of the seller without taking a cue from the competitive environment. This method, however, aims to specify the return on the producer's capital. Target return pricing can work in a competitive environment if the producer, starting with the market price, can design its cost structure so that it can sell at the competitive market price and still reap a forecast rate of profit.

## Price Skimming

Have you ever noticed that some new-to-the-world products initially carry a high price but the price gradually drops in the months that follow the launch? This pricing pattern is common in high-tech consumer products. It is often a function of underlying production economies, wherein the cost of the product drops precipitously as the manufacturer adds the capacity needed to satisfy demand *and* becomes increasingly effective in reducing costs.

But not always and not entirely. In some cases, a declining price is a manifestation of *price skimming*, a deliberate strategy through which the producer "skims" high profits from lead users—the people for whom the new product is a must-have item. You may recall what happened when shortwave car phones and then cell phones were introduced. Some people were willing to pay almost anything to have these new gadgets, either for reasons of utility or status.

Once profits have been skimmed off the must-have segment of the market, the producer drops the price and skims the next tier of interested customers. And on it goes. Each price drop broadens the market for the new product. Stereo sound systems, electronic calculators, personal computers, cell phones, digital cameras, flat screen monitors, and MP3 players have all followed this pricing pattern. Figure 9-1 tells the tale. Here, the vendor of a new and exciting consumer product prices it high and attracts a small but free-spending segment of people who must be the first in their neighborhoods to have the new product. Unit sales are small, but the high price makes the venture lucrative.

FIGURE 9-1

**Price skimming**

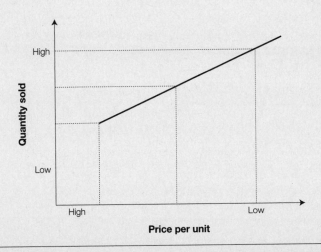

After the high-end market has been skimmed, the company lowers the price, thereby attracting a larger market and selling more units.

All the while, the company has been ramping up its production capacity, improving factory throughput, and gaining economies of scale. With per-unit manufacturing costs dropping, it can afford to lower its price again, and in doing so it makes the product attractive to a still larger but more price-sensitive market of customers. Unit sales grow. The relationship between price and quantity is indicated by the demand curve that touches each point in the figure. This assumes that there are different segments that will respond differently to price.

Price skimming is not always a good idea. For one thing, it invites competition. By holding the price at a high level while it skims profits from affluent customers who can afford to pay, the innovator creates an opportunity for a fast-following rival to enter the market at a lower price and grab large chunks of the market. If this happens, the innovator may find itself stranded in a small segment of the market that will soon be saturated. Concern about rivals is not an issue as long as the price skimmer enjoys a temporary monopoly. But some manufacturers of consumer products are expert at quickly copying new products in ways that do not violate patent protections.

## Penetration Pricing

*Penetration pricing* is a strategy that sets the initial price of a product (or service) lower than supply and demand conditions would dictate. Companies that adopt this strategy do so with the expectation that their product will be more widely accepted by the market: people who would otherwise not buy will buy, or people who are loyal to an established rival product will come over to their side.

Penetration pricing maximizes unit sales and produces gains in market share, but at the expense of profit margin. A low margin, however, is not always bad, because it can discourage entry by competitors. Consider this hypothetical example:

> *McSwiggin Electronics is the first to develop a new type of engineering software. Before launching this new product, company managers meet to*

*discuss pricing. One manager argues in favor of price skimming. "There's nothing like this on the market," he says. "Let's maximize our profits with a high price until someone comes out with a competing product."*

*Another manager argues in favor of a penetration price strategy. "Yes, a high initial price would let us maximize profits," she argues, "but that will simply encourage competition. Once our competitors see the price we're getting, they'll develop equivalent products. Before long there will be five or six competitors in the market, and none of us will be making money. If we maintain a low price and low margin, competitors will view the market as unattractive and will stay out."*

Penetration pricing is not free of negatives. After the price is established, raising the price may be difficult or impossible. Also, if you are not an efficient producer—that is, if you cannot continually lower production costs—you may be permanently locked in to a low-margin business. The experience of credit card and cell phone companies points to another problem: penetration pricing attracts lots of bargain hunters, and in the long run many of them will be unprofitable and will quickly drop out if you raise your price.

If you plan to follow a penetration pricing strategy, also develop a plan for cutting your production and distribution costs. That is your best assurance of obtaining a respectable profit margin, as shown in figure 9-2.

**FIGURE 9-2**

**Profitable penetration pricing depends on progressive cost reductions**

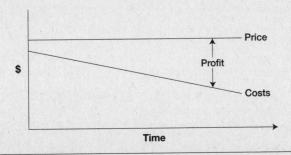

## Exploiting the Experience Curve

Another pricing strategy progressively lowers the price as you are able to lower your costs of production. It is based on the observable fact that people become more proficient as they repeat a task. Production managers know that people learn to do a job more quickly and with fewer errors the more often they do the job. Thus, a heart operation that once took eight hours can be done successfully in four hours as a surgical team gains experience with the procedure. Before long, they may have it completed in two or three hours. The same thing is observed in manufacturing settings when managers and employees focus on learning. Process improvement follows in the footsteps of learning.

The *experience curve* concept holds that the cost of doing a repetitive task decreases by some percentage each time the cumulative volume of production doubles. Thus, a company that climbs aboard the experience curve sooner than an imitator can theoretically maintain a cost advantage. Consider the two cost curves in figure 9-3. Companies A and B begin at the same cost level and learn at the same rate. They compete primarily on price. But A got into the game first and consequently is further down the cost curve than rival B, maintaining its cost advantage at every point in time. At time T, for example, that advantage is C.

Company A, having a clear cost advantage over its rival, can pass on some of its cost savings to buyers and still be profitable. And it can continue doing this as it continues down the experience curve. Company B, on the other hand, has little or no ability to cut prices and maintain profits. To be competitive, it must either learn to cut costs at a much faster rate, accept a permanent cost disadvantage (and smaller profit margin), or exit the market.

This experience curve strategy for pricing is appropriate for first-to-market companies that are also accomplished in the art of production. For these companies, this pricing tool progressively broadens demand for the product, because demand normally expands as price decreases. It is also a powerful barrier to entry as well

FIGURE 9-3

**The experience advantage**

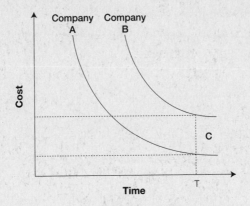

*Company A began sooner, so it reduces costs sooner than B, maintaining its cost advantage over time. At time T, for example, the advantage is C.*

as a method for squeezing the profit margins of rivals who get into the market late.

## Prestige Pricing

*Prestige pricing* aims to create a perception of brand quality or exclusivity in the minds of customers by setting a high price. Many people judge the quality of a product or service by the going price. For them, a reasonable price connotes acceptable quality; an exorbitant price embues the product or service with an aura of excellence and exclusivity. Packaging and advertising reinforce this perception, which, in many cases, is baseless. The cosmetics industry has elevated prestige pricing to the level of an art form.

Consider the case of a certain Asian vendor of women's cosmetics. In 2003, this company began advertising its new olive oil–based skin care product with lavish brochures that extolled the benefits of olive oil for the skin and featured plush photos of beautiful models and groves of olive trees. Its product retailed in the United States for $32 for a fancy bottle holding one fluid ounce. The contents of the bottle? A premium estate-bottled extra virgin olive oil from Spain.

What few buyers realized was that they could purchase the same oil from the same Spanish grower at their local food store for roughly $24 for a 17-ounce bottle—or about $1.41 per fluid ounce. Other oils that meet the same "extra virgin" standards (a measure of free fatty acids and processing without heat) can be readily had for much less! Packaging and advertising, in this case, were all that separated a supposedly premium item from a commonplace commodity.

But the power of prestige pricing is such that the producer would sell much less if it slashed its price. In this regard, the behavior of buyers runs counter to the economic law of demand, which states that demand increases as price decreases.

## Bait and Hook Pricing

A *bait and hook* pricing strategy sets the initial purchase price low but charges aggressively for replacement parts or other materials consumed in the course of using the product. The razor blade offers a familiar example.

Gillette has done well for its owners for more than a century, in part because of its success in selling replacement blades for its shaving devices. The prices on Gillette shavers are low, and they come with a small supply of replacement blades. After those blades are used up, of course, the customer must return to the store to buy more—and they aren't cheap. For example, in spring 2005 you could buy Gillette's Mach3 shaver for a mere $7.69 at a major U.S. drugstore chain. But twelve blade cartridges, roughly a two- to three-month supply for most men, went for $21.99.

Makers of ink-jet printers appear to have adopted the same pricing strategy: sell the printer cheaply, but make up for it on ink cartridges. You can buy a remarkably reliable and effective Hewlett-Packard ink-jet printer for less than $150—a real bargain. Canon and Epson offer similar deals. Replacement ink cartridges for these machines, however, are another story. Some cost as much as $52 each. For these companies, the profits are not in the machines but in the ink. A small office will spend more on ink cartridges in one year than it spent on the purchase of its printer.

The danger in this strategy is that a maker of generic replacement consumables will underprice them and steal a big part of the lucrative after-sale market—or, alternatively, force the incumbent to cut its own price. This strategy drains profits from the enterprise. We see this process at work today. Staples, the largest U.S. business supplies store chain, now offers its own HP-compatible ink cartridges for 25 percent less than HP, and a number of smaller companies sell cartridge refill kits for as little as $15. The only defense the printer makers have against these encroachments is to (1) warn customers that the use of off-brand cartridges may void the printer's warranty and (2) cut their own cartridge prices.

When you can't raise the bridge, sometimes you have to lower the water, as explained in "The Tricky Business of Raising Prices."

## Price Promotions

Marketers use *price promotions*—special, short-term deals that temporarily reduce the price or offer rebates—when they

- Introduce a new product or service

- Want to attract loyal users of another brand

- Must clear the distribution channel of excess inventory

Price promotions often take the form of coupons that customers can use to reduce the price at the cash register. For example, when packaged-food companies introduce new items, they encourage people to try them by distributing coupons worth, say, 50 cents off the retail price. Given the huge number of competing

## The Tricky Business of Raising Prices

One sales manager we know tells the story of how the previous generation of senior management raised prices. "Our president would take our product catalog and a red pen to the coffee room," he recalls. "He'd pour himself a cup and go through the list, arbitrarily crossing out current prices and writing in new, higher ones." That company, we learned, was not in a price-sensitive business; it managed to get away with this arbitrary approach for many years.

Because demand in most industries is price sensitive, the job of raising prices—even when doing so is justified by higher costs, inflation, and improvements in quality—should be approached with considerable caution. Many businesses simply mask the fact that they are raising prices. Consider these three examples:

- Knowing that ticket prices (already high) were a big issue with moviegoers, a threater chain kept ticket prices the same but raised prices on popcorn, soft drinks, and candy.

- Automakers are deathly afraid of raising sticker prices, so they are more likely to raise prices on factory- and dealer-installed options such as air conditioners, sound systems, and sun roofs. They also drop sales enticements such as zero-interest financing in an attempt to raise margins.

- In the tough times of the early 2000s, airlines discontinued customer perks such as free meals while keeping ticket prices steady.

Alternatively, companies wait for the industry leader to raise its prices, making it safe for them to boost theirs. How do companies in your industry handle price increases?

brands, this type of promotion is essential if the product is to be noticed by the buying public. Alternatively, customers may be offered a rebate. For example, Intuit, maker of the popular TurboTax software sold in the United States, offered a $14 rebate to purchasers of its deluxe version.

Price promotions can also be used in a defensive role: to prevent customer defection. The Shaw's supermarket chain has used price promotions to maintain customer loyalty when a competitor opens a store nearby. For example, when Market Basket, a small eastern Massachusetts chain, opened a new grocery store within a quarter-mile of the Shaw's store in Salem, Shaw's blanketed the area with coupons worth $6 off the purchase of $60 or more in groceries. Local households received three of these coupons, each redeemable during each of three succeeding weeks. Those weeks, not surprisingly, coincided with the opening of the new Market Basket store. The clear objective was to discourage Shaw's customers from visiting the rival store during its crucial "grand opening" period—and possibly switching their allegience. So, while Market Basket was promoting the opening of its new store, Shaw's was running a promotion to counter its rival's promotion.

Price promotions are also used to sell old or end-of-season merchandise and make way for new items. Users of the Apple Macintosh computer are surely familiar with the periodic "Mac Blow Out" price promotions that resellers use to clear their warehouses of overstock and of machines being superceded by new, improved models. Apparel stores do the same thing to clear out their seasonal clothing inventories.

The danger of price promotions is that employing them too often can produce undesirable consequences: customers devalue the regular price and delay their purchases until the next price promotion comes around. Other people learn to switch between brands and never become loyal users. Generally, the winners in price promotions are buyers. So too are vendors of weak brands that have nothing to lose and everything to gain. Vendors of established brands are seldom winners in the price promotion game.

# Customer–Perceived Value:
# The Ultimate Arbiter of Price

A marketer must understand how the individuals and committees who make purchase decisions assess value, because customer-perceived *value* is, in the end, the ultimate arbiter of pricing. Robert Dolan has used *true economic value* (TEV) as a conceptual yardstick to measure how customers calculate what they are willing to pay.[1] TEV is calculated as follows:

TEV = Cost of the Best Alternative + Value
of Performance Differential

TEV represents what a customer will actually pay for a product or service that delivers value in excess of its closest competitor. Consider this example:

*Helen needs to find a flight from Miami to Barcelona right away. She has just learned about an important three-day biotech conference beginning tomorrow afternoon, and she wants to participate in as many workshops and general sessions as possible. She has asked a travel agent to call her with available flights and fares.*

*The agent calls with this information. "There is a direct flight to Barcelona this evening. It will get you there in time for the opening of the conference. The price is $1,300 for a round trip. I also found another flight that leaves at about the same time. It has a three-hour layover in Madrid, so you'd arrive at the conference in the late afternoon. This is a coach seat, but it costs only $600 round trip."*

Helen has a clear choice; she can save $700 if she is willing to arrive three hours late. Is missing three hours of workshops worth the extra travel cost? One way to find out is to apply the TEV formula:

TEV = $600 + Value of Performance Differential

Helen, in this case, must estimate the value, to her, of attending three extra hours of the conference and the convenience of a direct flight. If that value is less than $700, the indirect flight represents the better deal. If she values the direct flight as worth the extra $700—or more—then $1,300 is the "right" price as far as Helen is concerned.

Marketers can use this same approach in determining a competitive market price for products that have added features or performance enhancements not available on existing products. Using customer surveys, for example, they can use an existing product as the cost of the alternative in the TEV formula; they ask survey subjects to place a value on the performance differential of their new product. For example, if existing 5-megapixel digital cameras are selling for $450, survey data could give marketers a sense of what customers would pay for a similar 5-megapixel camera that has an integrated water- and impact-resistant case. The same technique can be used to set prices on good, better, and best offerings within a company's product line.

Conjoint analysis, explained in chapter 3, is an even more powerful tool for determining what customers are willing to pay for perceived value differences. Conjoint analysis provides insights into the trade-offs that customers will make between alternatives.

No matter which approach you use to understand your customers' measures of value, you must recognize that value, like beauty, is in the eye of the beholder. For example, for a tourist traveling to Barcelona on vacation, a direct flight is probably not worth a $700 premium over an indirect flight via Madrid. Avoiding the three-hour layover is worth the added cost to a professional like Helen, but probably not to a vacationer. Similarly, a camera with a water- and impact-resistant case is much more valuable to an Alpine hiker than to someone who likes to take pictures of her children. So, in conducting customer price research, you should be very clear about which market segment you plan to target.

## Pricing and the Product Life Cycle

From a strategic point of view, the product life cycle provides a framework for thinking about pricing decisions. Recall figure 1-3, which identified four phases in the product life cycle: introduction,

growth, maturity, and decline. Each phase presents different opportunities and constraints on price.

### Introduction Phase

During the introduction phase, pricing can be a quandary, especially
if you enjoy a temporary monopoly. In that situation, there may be
no direct competitor and thus no benchmark for what buyers will
tolerate or for their sensitivity to price differences. There may be in-
direct competitors (substitutes), however, and you can use them as
starting points for the pricing decision.

That brings us back to the total economic value equation,
wherein the price of the best alternative is known but the value of
the performance differential of the new product is unknown. Customers themselves may have difficulty in sizing up the value of
something that is new and different. They too lack benchmarks of
value. In such instances you can adopt any of these strategies:

- **Skimming.** Some people will be happy to pay a high price for
  anything that is new and unique. This strategy, of course, is
  short term and contains dangers, as described earlier.

- **Penetration pricing.** A low price may have the threefold benefit
  of (1) establishing you as the market share champion, (2) dis-
  couraging market entry by competitors, and (3) creating broad-
  based demand for the product.

- **Cost–plus.** In a monopoly, the producer can administer its own
  price, and cost-plus is one way of determining that price. Just
  remember, however, that product monopolies are short-lived.

Pricing decisions in this introductory phase are not only difficult
but also deadly important. Putting too high a price on a newly introduced product may kill it in its infancy, undoing the work of
many employees over a long period of development.

### Growth Phase

The growth phase is characterized by increasing unit sales and accelerating customer interest. How should you set the price in this situ-

ation? If competitors have not yet surfaced (an unlikely event), skimming may be appropriate. All the deep-pocketed buyers who simply had to be the first in their neighborhoods to own the product have already been skimmed in the introduction phase. So now you must gradually reduce prices, skimming other market segments that are progressively more price sensitive.

A producer that enjoys prime position on the experience curve will also want to progressively reduce prices during this phase. Doing so will maintain its margins even as the strategy expands unit sales and punishes late-into-the-game rivals. Some of these rivals will either take a loss on every sale or throw in the towel.

### Mature Phase

By the time a product enters this phase, growth in unit sales is leveling off and the remaining competitors are trying to find ways to differentiate their products. During this phase we begin to see sellers offer different versions of the product, each version trying to colonize a targeted segment. Price is one of the factors used in this strategy (e.g., by developing and pricing good, better, and best versions to expand the product line).

### Decline

Competition gets ugly in this phase. Total demand for the product category is now visibly slipping, perhaps because of the appearance of superior substitutes or because of market saturation. Whatever the case, you can see the handwriting on the wall: unit sales will continue to decline. Some companies will get out of the business entirely; those that remain will aggressively try to take business away from their rivals.

Everyone is trying to harvest as much as possible from a contracting market. Price tactics include the following:

- Beat a retreat on price, but work overtime to reduce production costs. Success in the latter will maintain a decent profit margin.
- Increase the price on the few remaining units in inventory. This may sound like a sure way to drive all customers away, but there may be a small number of customers who still rely on

that particular product. This is particularly true of replacement parts. Here the seller hopes that the higher price will compensate for fewer sales. When the inventory is exhausted, the product line is terminated.

Pricing is one of the linchpins of marketing strategy and success. How is your company making its pricing decisions? Are these decisions appropriate for the current phase of the product life cycle? The most reliable method of pricing is to get inside the heads of customers, because how they value your products relative to those of competitors and substitutes matters more than anything else.

## Summing Up

- Price strategy is usually motivated by a specific objective: maximizing profits, maximizing unit sales, gaining market share, and the like.

- Cost-plus pricing is appropriate only in noncompetitive markets.

- A price skimming strategy initially sets the price high. It aims to skim high profits from the small market segment for whom the product or service is a must-have. Once that segment has been satisfied, the price is reduced progressively to make the item attractive to other, more price-sensitive segments.

- Penetration pricing sets the price low with the goal of gaining market share leadership. A low price makes the market unattractive to potential rivals, but also results in small profit margins.

- The experience curve reflects a producer's ability to learn how to reduce time and cost as production increases. The first company on the experience curve enjoys a cost advantage over latecomers, allowing it to reduce prices but continue making a profit.

- The aim of prestige pricing is to use a high price to create a perception of brand quality or exclusivity.

- Sometimes referred to as the razor blade strategy, bait and hook pricing sets the initial purchase price low but charges aggressively for replacement parts or other materials consumed in using the product: examples are razor blades, ink-jet cartridges, and so forth. The main threat to the strategy is the existence of generic replacements.

- Raising prices is risky in a highly competitive field unless the market share leader does so first. Producers can reduce the risk by keeping the price the same but raising prices of repairs and replacement parts. The elimination of low-interest financing and free perks is another way of raising the price without drawing the attention of buyers.

- Price promotions are used most often when producers are attempting to introduce a new item or service, trying to attract buyers from competing brands, and attempting to clear old merchandise from the distribution channel.

- In a free and open market, customer-perceived value is the ultimate arbiter of price.

- Each phase of the product life cycle presents a different pricing challenge and opportunity.

# Integrated Marketing Communications

*Creativity, Consistency, and Effective Resource Allocation*

## Key Topics Covered in This Chapter

- *The six steps of the purchase decision*

- *Characteristics of key communication vehicles*

- *The six M's of market communications*

- *Guidelines for coordinating marketing communications*

MANAGERS HAVE ALWAYS had to face the challenge of creating awareness among targeted customers and bringing them to the point of interest and confidence when they will reach for their wallets and make a purchase. Over the years various forms of marketing communications have been used for this purpose: media advertising, personal selling, direct mail, and so forth. Web marketing is a recent addition to this communications mix.

With people receiving so many messages from so many sources, managers face a new challenge: producing a consistent brand message at each customer touch point. The answer to this challenge is a strategic process generally known as *integrated marketing communications* (IMC). IMC's goal is to use multiple modes of communication to foster awareness of a company's products or services, inform people about features and benefits, and move them to make a purchase. Those multiple modes must be consistent and complementary.

This chapter explains the goals of IMC and describes six steps you can take to achieve them. It also provides a conceptual overview of the many types of market communication vehicles and their differences in two important dimensions. The great challenge to managers is to understand how best to allocate scarce marketing resources among these vehicles and to ensure that they are working in a coordinated and consistent manner.

# The Goal of Marketing Communications

The ultimate goal of marketing communications is to influence someone to make a purchase. But like most goals, it is attainable only through a number of process steps. Consider these:

1. **Create awareness.** People will not buy a product or service that they are not aware of. Consequently, companies go to great lengths to create awareness. For example, when Amtrak initiated its Acela Express rail service from Boston to New York City, it blanketed the two cities' airways and newspapers with ads announcing the new, high-speed service.

2. **Provide knowledge.** This step involves providing information about product or service features. What is the product? What does it do? Amtrak described Acela's amenities and schedule: electrical outlets for laptops and DVD players, adjustable lighting, conference tables, a club car. "Trains depart from Boston's South Station at . . ."

3. **Create a favorable impression.** People don't buy features; instead, they buy benefits—things that will make their lives better, solve a nagging problem, or save them money. The Acela boasted two customer benefits: it would move passengers from city center to city center in comfort *and* would allow them to work productively throughout the trip.

4. **Attain a preferred position in the customer's mind.** "Take the Acela Express and you will miss airport hassles, cramped seats, long security lines, weather delays, and cancellations." To many stressed-out business travelers along the Boston to New York corridor, this positioning moved rail travel ahead of air travel.

5. **Create a purchase intention.** If the marketer has done a good job of addressing earlier steps in the process, the customer will

resolve to make a purchase. "I'm going to New York for a conference next month. This time I'll try the Acela."

6. **Make the sale.** If all the other steps have been completed, the prospect will become a customer. The cash register will ring.

Those are the steps that typically lead to a purchase. An alternative is to use market research to classify targeted customers in the following order: (1) is unaware of our product; (2) is aware of the product but considers it similar to others being considered; (3) is favorably disposed to our product; (4) would select our product if the purchase were made today; and (5) buys our product.

Whichever set of steps you use, the job of IMC is to move targeted customers to the act of buying the product or service.

## Communication Vehicles

A marketer with a generous budget has access to an arsenal of communication options: electronic media (TV and radio), print media (newspapers and magazines), direct mail solicitations, telemarketing, personal selling, and the Web. Even public relations is a means of communicating with current and potential customers.

As a consumer, you are surely familiar with each of these avenues. By some estimates, individual Americans are exposed to fifteen hundred to sixteen hundred commercial messages during a typical day: radio and TV commercials, ads in the morning newspaper, billboards along the highway, solicitations in the mail, calls from telemarketers, Web page banners, and even the guy who tries to sell you a counterfeit Rolex watch as you walk out of the subway station. The magnitude of contemporary communication clutter is such that people have learned to tune out all except a small percentage of commercial messages; perhaps 5 percent is even noticed. An even smaller percentage can be associated with an actual sale.

How do you cut through the clutter and move the prospective customer further along the purchase decision process—from awareness on the front end to an actual purchase? This is the question that everyone involved in sales and advertising must answer.

Conceptually, we can categorize the vehicles of marketing communications in two dimensions, as shown in figure 10-1. The first dimension, shown on the vertical axis, relates to targeting and customization. At the top end of this axis are communications that address an individual prospect whose needs and interests you already know. A direct mail catalog of carpentry tools sent to members of the North American Carpenters Federation is an example of a highly targeted, customized communication. Another example is a salesperson's visit with the purchasing manager of an auto parts supplier.

On the other extreme we have mass communications, as in a TV commercial that runs on network TV during the final game of the World Series. That ad will be watched by millions of people—an undifferentiated cross section of society. As a practical matter, the

**FIGURE 10-1**

**Communication vehicles**

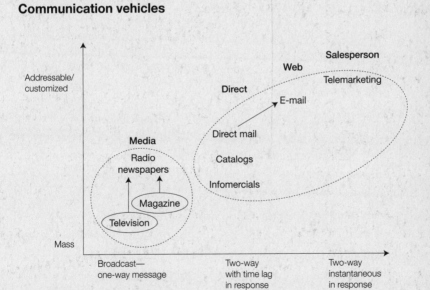

*Source:* Robert J. Dolan "Integrated Marketing Communications," Note 9-599-087 (Boston: Harvard Business School), revised June 1, 2000, 4. Adapted with permission.

commercial cannot be targeted to individual viewers or customized in any way.

Now consider the horizontal axis, which is divided into one-way and two-way communication, with an intermediate section. A TV commercial is strictly a one-way message; it can create awareness, and it may impart information about the features and benefits of the product, but not much else. The salesperson's visit with the purchasing manager, in contrast, is a two-way conversation in which the salesperson can describe his wares and the buyer can describe her particular needs and her reservations about pricing or terms, and can ask for specific information. The salesperson and the buyer can negotiate and perhaps conclude with a transaction. This two-way communication is effective in moving the buyer along the final steps of the purchasing process.

Notice the section between one-way and two-way communication. Here we find Web-based communication, direct mail, and TV infomercials. These have some characteristics of both one- and two-way communication. When you receive an L.L. Bean catalog, for example, it's essentially a one-way communication. However, you can call the 800 number listed on every page and speak with a customer representative about the products that most interest you.

### Where Public Relations Fits In

*Public relations* (PR) is a form of communication that aims to increase public awareness and understanding of, and to promote a favorable opinion of, a company, its products, and its services. PR tools include press releases, speeches by executives, and public service activities. Unlike other forms of communication, PR operates through unpaid channels. Consequently, you have no control over how your PR efforts will play out. If you take out a half-page ad in *Forbes*, you control when it will appear and what it will say. In contrast, a press release announcing your development of a new, faster computer chip may not be picked up by the press, and, if it is, the article may not tout the development in the way you would hope.

The primary virtue of PR in marketing communications is casting the company in a favorable light among the general public. Some of that aura can be expected to adhere to the company's products and services.

### Selecting the Right Communication Vehicles

Given the many communication vehicles currently available, along with their characteristics, which are right for your product or service? Here are two tips for choosing an approach.

First, consider how far along your potential customers are in the purchasing process. Are they aware of your product or service? If they are, how much do they know about its benefits for them? For those who know these things, are you in the preferred position or a second choice behind a rival?

Chances are that you'll find prospective customers in every one of the purchase process steps, although they may be concentrated at certain points. Simply understanding where they are can help you make decisions about the communication vehicles you'll use to carry your message. For example, if awareness is a big issue and if your product is for golfers, you might consider The Golf Channel on cable TV or a print ad in a golf magazine. These media present opportunities to raise awareness and create name recognition.

If your audience is highly targeted and if most of your potential customers are near the end of the purchasing process, personal selling is usually most effective in moving them toward a transaction. For example, suppose the maker of fuel injectors knows that its product is among the three being considered by the purchasing manager of an engine manufacturer. A personal sales call is the best approach to getting the order.

Second, use the most highly targeted vehicles you can. Unless your product or service aims to appeal to a broad, heterogeneous cross section of the public, use one-way or two-way vehicles that you can customize for prospective customers. This approach will give you better results for the least amount of money. Business-to-business markets should put the lion's share of their resources into these targeted vehicles.

## Putting It All Together

As a marketer, you face the challenge of communicating with customers in a way that moves them toward a purchase. As you do so, keep these points—the six M's—in mind:[1]

1. **Market.** To whom is your communication addressed? Remember that your market may include final customers *and* the retailers or wholesalers through which your products are sold.

2. **Mission.** What is your objective in communicating?

3. **Message.** What specific points must be communicated? Final customers may be interested only in the features and benefits of the product; intermediaries, on the other hand, will be more interested in the terms of trade, the reliability of delivery, volume discounts, and your efforts to generate demand through advertising.

4. **Media.** Which communication vehicles should you use to get the message across? One medium is seldom enough.

5. **Money.** How much will be budgeted for the effort?

6. **Measurement.** How will you assess the impact of your communication? Management will be more generous with funds if you have a solid plan for measuring results.

Point 4, media, bears further discussion. In many cases your communication will aim at more than one market and will involve more than one communication vehicle. In fact, you may need to use different messages and different means to address people who are in the different purchasing process steps. To appreciate why more than one vehicle is often needed, consider this hypothetical example:

*Dearie Bear Candy Company uses mass media advertising, direct mail, a nationwide cadre of sales representatives, and a Web site to com-*

*municate with its market. Its public relations department also gets into the act.*

*Dearie Bear runs TV commercials in the weeks leading up to the various holidays and special occasions for which people buy candy—primarily Easter, Mother's Day, Halloween, and Christmas. These ads energize demand by extolling the virtues of Dearie Bear candies and telling viewers that they can buy them "wherever fine candies are sold." Long before these ads run, the company's commissioned sales reps are busy visiting buyers at supermarket and convenience store chains, mass-market retailers, and large confection stores. They want to be sure that retail sellers are stocked to meet the demand created by the TV ads. Thus, advertising and personal selling work hand in hand. Each addresses a different audience. Another sales team, based at the company's headquarters, works with nonprofit organizations that make Dearie Bear candies part of their community fund-raising campaigns.*

*Dearie Bear also sends 100,000 catalogs and direct mail ads to its mailing list of buyers in the course of a year. These ads encourage retailers to reorder between sales visits via the company's 800 number, or through Dearie Bear's state-of-the-art Web site.*

*Not leaving anything to chance, the company's PR department regularly sends out press releases announcing the donation of Dearie Bear products to veterans' hospitals and charitable organizations around the country. These are meant to create name recognition and a positive public image for Dearie Bear and its products.*

In this example, the company is using mass-market advertising to create awareness, to make Dearie Bear candies the preferred choice, and to drive consumers into the stores. But it is using much more targeted, two-way communication to ensure that the stores will stock enough of the product to satisfy consumer demand.

## The Management Challenge

Marketing managers have an important two-part challenge with respect to IMC: (1) finding the best way to allocate financial resources in support of their brands and (2) coordinating their spending so that all customer touch points are getting consistent messages.

In a simpler time, brand managers could allocate a large chunk of their budgets to an advertising or media agency and direct the rest to internally controlled promotion. Today, because channels of distribution and customer communication are so many and so varied, managers must optimize resource allocation among *all* the activities that touch customers: packaging, point-of-sale display and promotion, Web-based selling, and ad agency work. They may find themselves pulled in different directions by the advice of brand consultants, direct marketing agencies, e-commerce advisers, and after-sales support.

Managers must also ensure that each of these activities represents the product to customers in a consistent manner. The worst thing that can happen is to have TV advertising saying that the company's new breakfast cereal is a healthy choice for adult tastes when, at the same time, a design firm is creating a cereal box that makes the product seem like fun food for children. Such inconsistencies confuse customers and undermine brands.

One practical way to avoid inconsistency is to put yourself in the customer's shoes as you review the IMC program. Do the messages aimed at customers create a clear, consistent, and attractive picture of the product? Are the physical characteristics of the product, its point-of-sale presentation, and the look of media advertising and direct mail pieces consistent? Do they reinforce one another? Apple Computer, by one poll the most powerful brand in North America, provides a great example of excellence in this area. The shape and feel of the company's products, its logo, and every piece of advertising tell you, "It's an Apple." There's no mistaking it. This is what you need to achieve in your marketing communications.

## Summing Up

- Integrated marketing communications (IMC) is a strategic process for producing a consistent brand message at each customer touch point. Its goal is to use multiple modes of communication to foster awareness of a company's products or services, inform people about features and benefits, and move them to make a purchase.

- Effective IMC provides messages that are consistent and complementary.

- Marketing communications aims to create awareness, provide knowledge, create a favorable impression, attain a preferred position in the customer's mind, create a purchase intention, and make the sale.

- It is useful to think of communication vehicles along two dimensions: targeted versus scattered, and one-way versus two-way.

- In choosing communication vehicles, consider where potential customers are in the purchasing process. Then use the most highly targeted vehicles you can.

- Marketing managers should (1) find the best way to allocate financial resources in support of their brands and (2) coordinate that spending so that all customer touch points receive consistent messages.

# Interactive Marketing

*New Channel, New Challenge*

## Key Topics Covered in This Chapter

- *The rising tide of online commerce*

- *E-mail campaigns and best practices*

- *Web-based merchandising best practices*

**T**HE TERM *Internet marketing* refers to any activity that uses the Internet to advertise and sell goods and services to consumers, business, or nonprofit organizations and government. At the highest level, the traditional issues of marketing apply. Like their offline cousins, online marketers must give the same attention to product, price, and promotion. They must think just as deeply about segmenting, targeting, positioning, creating awareness, building traffic, and motivating people to buy.

As one Web marketing expert put it, Internet marketing is "a daily grind of doing lots and lots of simple things well. It's about being useful. It's about creating a Web site that is convenient and fast."[1] The element that differs more than anything else from traditional marketing is "place," for the Internet represents a new and unique channel of distribution. This chapter examines the two key forms of Internet marketing: e-mail and Web-based merchandising.

## Growing Online Sales

The online sales of consumer and business products have grown tremendously in recent years, and that growth is forecast to continue (see "Areas of Fastest Online Retail Growth"). On the retail side,

## Areas of Fastest Online Retail Growth

A study conducted by Forrester Research on behalf of Shop.org, a unit of the National Retail Federation, projected the most rapidly growing categories of retail online sales for 2005.

|  | Projected growth rate | Projected total sales (2005) |
|---|---|---|
| Travel | 20% | $62.8 billion |
| Cards and gifts | 30% | $4.8 billion |
| Cosmetics and fragrances | 33% | $1.6 billion |
| Jewelry and luxury items | 28% | $3.2 billion |

SOURCE: Mylene Mangalinda, "Online Retail Sales Are Expected to Rise to $172 Billion This Year," *Wall Street Journal*, May 24, 2005, D5.

2004 U.S. online retail sales reached more than $89 billion—$26 billion during the Christmas holiday season alone—and Jupiter Research has forecast that those sales will continue to grow at a compound annual rate of 17 percent through 2008. Others forecast an even higher rate of growth. As if to confirm that rosy outlook, first-quarter 2005 online sales in the United States leaped 24 percent above sales during the same period of 2004, according to the U.S. Department of Commerce.

Although 2004 Internet sales account for only about 5 percent of total U.S. retail sales for that year, they may represent only the tip of the iceberg as far as the Internet's influence on buying behavior is concerned. It is generally believed that 30 percent of all purchases made in bricks-and-mortar retail stores are influenced by prepurchase research conducted on the Internet. In other words, millions of consumers obtain information, read product descriptions and reviews, and compare prices online before they go to a store to make a purchase.[2]

What is happening in the consumer world is mirrored on the B2B (business-to-business) front, where billions of dollars' worth of transactions are now being made over the Internet, often through online auctions. Suppliers bid against each other to provide manufacturers with everything from raw materials to finished components.

Rising online sales are a consequence of several factors. First, each year more people are using the Internet, and they are growing accustomed to comparing products and prices and placing orders. Second, once these buyers get comfortable with buying via the Internet, they make more of their purchases online. Finally, increasing numbers of companies are creating e-commerce sites and launching e-mail marketing campaigns (see "Marketers Are Investing Heavily").

Internet marketing offers several benefits for sellers:

- It neutralizes geographic boundaries. Bricks-and-mortar venders are limited to customers who live within driving distance. For goods that are downloadable or easily shipped, the Internet opens the market to customers anywhere in the world. For example, a seller of classic automobiles was limited to buyers in and around his Los Angeles dealership. Today, buyers from thousands of miles away purchase his autos through eBay auctions, some for more than $60,000.

- Internet users have above-average household incomes—the population that many sellers cherish.

- The cost of reaching potential buyers is much smaller online. The variable cost of a customer contact via e-mail is about $0.02. Doing the same with direct mail costs twenty-five to fifty times as much. E-mail's low contact cost makes the sale of low-priced items feasible, particularly when those items can be directly downloaded by customers.

- The Internet is a convenient medium through which to communicate and maintain long-term relationships with customers.

## Marketers Are Investing Heavily

Online marketing was a huge buzz in the late 1990s, but when the Internet bubble burst, interest subsided. At least, that's the impression you'd get by observing the research agenda of the Marketing Science Institute. Each year this organization asks its practitioner members to identify areas of marketing that its scholar members should study. In the years just before the bubble burst, Internet marketing ranked at or near the top of the list. After 2000, it hasn't even made the top ten.

But there is a contradiction here. According to data compiled by the MET Report of the London Business School, Internet marketing investments continue to grow. They accounted for 7.7 percent of total marketing investments in 2003, and that figure was predicted to increase by 11.6 percent in 2004—at least three times the increases made in other marketing activities (media advertising, direct mail, etc.). The MET Report concludes that "the recent growth in interactive marketing is, if anything, accelerating and is likely to continue long-term."

Thus, even though initial exuberance about this form of marketing has subsided, investments in it have not. This is not surprising inasmuch as people who access the Internet are doing so at the expense of other media, where marketers have traditionally spent their money. A 2005 study by BURST! Media, for example, indicates that Internet users report spending more time online—and less time with other media. Some 35 percent of Internet users said that they were watching less TV, and more than 30 percent said they were spending less time reading newspapers and magazines.

SOURCES: Patrick Barwise and Alan Styler, "Marketing Expenditure report predicts spending upturn and increased reliance on interactive media," London Business School, 16 December 2003, www.london.edu/ assets/documents/PDF/MET_Report_Exec_Summary_2.pdf. "Statistics: U.S Internet Usage," www.shop .org/learn/stats_usnet_general.asp.

# E-mail Marketing

E-mail marketing is a low-cost means of delivering messages to existing and targeted potential customers. These messages may have a number of goals:

- To make a sale.

- To maintain relationships with existing customers.

- To drive people to the vendor's e-commerce site or physical store for a sale. (One vendor interviewed for this chapter reported that 300,000 different individuals visited its site in a typical month, many driven by e-mail. Collectively, these individuals purchased $10 million in products during the year.)

- To build a brand through name recognition.

- To test an offer with a small sample of potential customers.

- To capture names and e-mail addresses by asking potential customers to opt in to the vendor's list.

A well-designed e-mail campaign can achieve many of these goals simultaneously—and produce an excellent return on investment. United Airlines, for example, sends its frequent flyer enrollees a monthly update of their account activity. This not only saves printing and mailing costs but also reminds the airline's customers, "We're here and eager to continue serving you." That same e-mail piece announces new routes ("Introducing our Chicago-Munich route"), new services, and special deals ("Earn 1,000 bonus miles"). A conspicuous link takes the curious reader to "My Mileage Plus," which contains an expanded set of announcements and offers. It's easy to click from that location to United's home page and its reservation tools.

## Names and Addresses Are the Key

Of the many things that e-mail marketers must do well, building an up-to-date list of the right people may be the most critical. By "right people" we mean people who have a natural interest in what you are selling and have the capacity to buy. There are two ways to build such a list: opting in and purchasing lists.

OPTING IN. The first and best approach to building a list is to encourage current customers and site visitors to *opt in*. In Web commerce lingo, a person opts in by registering for free e-mail or a free newsletter. Opting in is facilitated by a notice on the company's home page, as shown in figure 11-1.

Clicking the Subscribe Now! link takes site visitors to a page where they are asked to provide name, postal address, e-mail address, and an indication of their preferences for future e-mail messages (see figure 11-2).

Potential customers who volunteer their name, address, and—best of all—purchase interests are worth their weight in gold to the marketer who aims to build a powerful list. However, you will receive this information only if you offer something of value in return: user tips, a relevant and well-crafted e-mail newsletter, or something similar.

PURCHASING LISTS. You can also build an e-mail list by purchasing names and e-mail addresses from list vendors and from organizations whose members interest you. But as in direct mail, the

---

**FIGURE 11-1**

**Sample opt-in Web page notice**

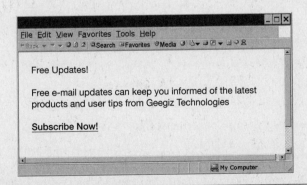

FIGURE 11-2

**Sample subscription Web page**

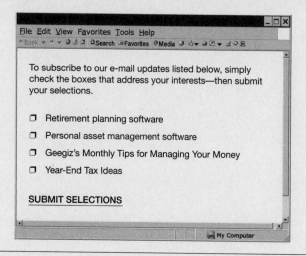

quality of purchased lists tends to be low because few organizations will share information on valued customers. Also, because people change their e-mail addresses frequently—much more frequently than their postal addresses—purchased lists are likely to be out of date. Thus, the best advice for building a high-quality list is to gather the names and addresses yourself.

## About Spam

Between 1937—when it was first introduced by Hormel—and very recently, Spam meant "spiced ham" packaged in a 12-ounce can. In the e-mail age, *spam* means something else: unrequested and un-wanted e-mail that is neither appetizing nor welcomed by recipients and legitimate e-mail merchants. Most of this junk mail is spewed out by computer robots, and often from scam artists. An estimated 2 billion such messages are sent each year. According to U.K. antispam software company Sophos, the top three countries of origin for spam are the United States (36 percent), South Korea (25 percent), and China (9 percent).

Internet service providers and their users have responded with antispam software. This software contains gatekeepers that look for telltale signs of spam: words such as *Free* and *Viagra*, and any words spelled in capital letters. Gatekeepers also bounce back messages that have problematic HTML construction. These safeguards have had the unwanted effect of blocking many legitimate e-mail messages—perhaps 15–20 percent—to recipients who have opted in. Even at the low cost of each e-mail sent, that's a substantial marketing investment down the drain. Perhaps as bad, the spam glut has trained many Internet users to delete commercial e-mail messages from all sources without reading them. This means still more marketing dollars down the drain.

To rein in spam, the U.S. government implemented the CAN-SPAM Act in January 2004. CAN-SPAM prohibits senders from hiding their identities with false headers and forbids the use of deceptive subject lines that lure the unsuspecting into opening spam messages. In addition, the law requires senders to post a valid physical address and prominently post a mechanism for opting out of future soliciations. Opt-out requests must be processed within ten business days.

Many of the U.S. states have their own antispam laws. In April 2005, Virginia made its first felony conviction of a major spammer who had sent at least 10 million solicitations per year over sixteen phone lines under various aliases. According to prosecutors, the spammer was selling junk products and pornography—and grossing almost $750,000 *per month*.[3] With potential rewards like this, it is little wonder that so many spammers have infested the Internet.

### Best Practices

E-mail can be an effective part of your marketing plan if handled responsibly and with care. Here are some of the recommended best practices:

• Team up with an experienced and savvy e-mail host company. The host is an outside vendor who handles the technology. A good one can reduce bounce-backs (messages that don't get through) and advise you as to the most effective content and optimal frequency of your messages.

- Have a contact strategy. Don't become a pest in the eyes of re-cipients. Many successful e-mail campaigners limit their fre-quency to one message per week.

- Give people an incentive to opt in. People are looking for value, not more advertising. Opting in should have a tangible payoff for targeted customers.

- Personalize your message to the greatest extent possible. Per-sonized messages get four to eight times as many responses, ac-cording to Jupiter Research.

- Avoid the appearance of spam. This means identifying yourself to recipients and avoiding the word *FREE* and other capital-ized words.

- Enhance your brand. A strong brand name produces sales through all channels, including e-mail.

## Web–Based Merchandising

The World Wide Web has been a godsend to busy consumers who need hard-to-find products quickly, and to all buyers—consumer and industrial—who want to compare products and find the best prices. Do you want to find the cheapest fare to Genoa on May 1? Check the Web. Do you need technical data and purchase informa-tion on fire-resistant materials for your next building project? The 3M site will give you the details on its products in just a few clicks.

Yes, the Web is a handy tool for buyers, and what's good for buy-ers has, by and large, been good for sellers, providing the following commercial benefits:

- It gives you an opportunity to sell directly, capturing the full margin that would otherwise be split with middlemen. In some businesses, the Web can also eliminate the need to maintain costly retail facilities.

- It lets you capture the names and addresses of the right customers through voluntary opt-in inducements. The very fact that a person has entered your site usually indicates an interest in your products.

- It reduces your human resource costs through self-service site features. For example, if you provide clear instructions for order submission, customers will do many of the chores that would otherwise be handled by customer service operators.

- A well-designed site can serve multiple markets and support many product lines.

- It presents cross-selling opportunities. Amazon.com's "You may also like . . ." and "Customers who bought this book also bought . . ." features are excellent examples of cross-selling on the Web.

- It lets you sell abroad at low cost. One U.S. company interviewed for this chapter reports growing sales of its downloadable printed materials to customers in India. Traditional distribution approaches would make those sales uneconomical.

Yes, the benefits of a well-designed e-commerce site are many, and they can far outstrip the associated costs over time. Those costs include the high up-front cost of building the site; the ongoing costs of hosting, making incremental improvements, and updating product information; and the cost of servicing orders.

## Best Practices

Many in the trade point to Amazon.com as a best-practice leader in consumer e-commerce because of its detailed systems for tracking customer preferences. The company goes beyond collecting information on actual purchases; it keeps tabs on what customers browsed but did not buy, and what items they recommended to others. Its search engine, A9, remembers every item for which every customer has searched. It knows the interests of people returning to its site and uses that knowledge to recommend specific items to individual site visitors.

Beyond the development of customer profiles, e-commerce practitioners point to the following best practices:

- **Search engine and keyword optimization.** Thoughtful assignment of keywords to your products and services ensures that your site will show up when shoppers run a Google search. The goal should be to have your site appear on the first or second page of a Google search. This is one of the keys to success online.

- **Targeted advertising, e–mails, and links on appropriate Web pages.** These Web-only vehicles drive likely buyers to the site.

- **Reciprocal links that build traffic on your site.** *Reciprocal links* are links with other sites that are generally related to your offering but not direct competitors. For example, if you had a women's apparel site but did not sell jewelry, you might want to have a reciprocal link arrangement with a jewelry site. Some of the people who visit that site will click through to yours, and vice versa. The best part is that these reciprocal deals are usually free.

- **Relevant content, including free content and previews.** These are particularly effective in getting visitors to voluntarily opt in to e-mail lists.

- **Easy–in, easy navigation, and easy–out site features.** Site design should reflect how customers want to use the site.

- **Accurate, compelling, and detailed product information.** Site visitors want sufficient detail so that they can be certain of what they'll be getting; otherwise, they don't buy. Also, your product information should be easily located through public and on-site search engines.

- **Saying "Thanks" and confirming transactions via e–mail after each purchase.**

- **Flawless fulfillment.** Fulfillment errors take the profits out of sales and alienate customers, so aim for zero-defect fulfillment.

Best practice also includes continuous improvement. Managers have plenty of opportunities to learn from and improve their sites. Everything can be measured: how many people are visiting and buying, what percentage are browsing but not buying, which pages are most popular, and so forth. This information, combined with brainstorming and observation of other sites, can give you ideas for incremental improvement. A series of incremental improvements can add up to major performance improvements over time.

You should also think beyond small, incremental improvements to the next generation of site design. Changing technology and changes in the business usually dictate a total redesign at some future point. Total redesign is expensive and eats up thousands of hours. But starting with a clean slate has many benefits. The design team can build on a foundation of the most current techology and functionality, and they can incorporate everything they have learned about customer preferences and the needs of various product lines.

So far, Internet marketing has failed to reach the heights predicted by earlier boosters and prognosticators. The parking lots around Wal-Mart, Borders booksores, and shopping malls are still packed. But Internet-based sales are substantial and growing. What are you doing to capture customers and build relationships through Internet marketing?

## Summing Up

- E-mail and Web-based merchandising are the two key forms of Internet marketing.

- E-mail campaigns can be used to make sales, build customer relationships, and drive people to Web sites and stores.

- Web-based merchandising gives vendors a direct link with customers, eliminating middlemen and costly retail facilities.

- Thoughtful keywording of products and services ensures that a site will show up when shoppers run a Google search.

# Marketing Across Borders

*It's a Big, Big World*

## Key Topics Covered in This Chapter

- *Standardized versus customized products and promotions*

- *Successes and failure among "world" products*

- *Approaches to distribution*

- *Control of global marketing decisions*

G LOBAL TRADE IS large and growing. In 2004 the United States alone exported more than $1.1 trillion in goods and services and imported almost $1.8 trillion. Global trade can also be profitable. U.S. companies, for example, raked in $315 billion in overseas profits during 2004, according to the U.S. Bureau of Economic Analysis. That amount was up 26 percent from 2003 and far outpaced profit growth from domestic operations.

Growth in global trade has been facilitated by better and cheaper communications, improved shipping, rising incomes in formerly poor regions, the removal of many trade restrictions, and the rise of manufacturing in places such as South Korea and China. Indeed, China's booming steel industry has created such demand for raw materials that iron ore mines in northern Minnesota—half a world away from the blast furnaces—have sprung back to life after decades of decline.

If they are not doing so already, companies look over their ramparts and wonder, Should we be marketing abroad? Could we? As with all marketing questions, the answers should be based on solid research and analysis—the same type of opportunity-seeking analysis described earlier in this book. You should ask yourself these questions:

- Which foreign markets are most attractive?

- Which segments of those markets are most feasible, given our current strengths? Are these segments stable or growing?

- What are the risks?

- How would we distribute our products?

- Must we alter our products to satisfy local preferences?

- How can we communicate effectively with people of different cultures?

Global marketing is a big subject—too big to be covered in this overview book. Consequently, our goal here is to examine a limited number of the issues that face any company considering marketing abroad, using the marketing mix as a reliable guide.

Earlier, we described the four P's of the marketing mix—product, place, price, and promotion—as the tools companies use to pursue their objectives in target markets. Fortunately, these tools are as useful in global commerce as they are in domestic commerce. This chapter revisits elements of the marketing mix and discusses their relevance to marketing across borders.

## Product Decisions

Twenty years ago, market watchers were predicting a homogenization of products around the globe, and there was plenty of evidence to support that view. North Americans were listening to music on the same Sony Walkman audio players as their counterparts in Japan. Businesses in Europe, Latin America, and Asia were building IT departments on IBM mainframe computers, and people everywhere were drinking Coca-Cola, shaving with Gillette razors, and wearing American blue jeans.

It seemed as though the tastes and desires of people in different countries and cultures were bound to converge. Marketing sage Theodore Levitt articulated this view in a classic 1983 *Harvard Business Review* article, "The Globalization of Markets."[1] Of course, not every product could cross borders. Gas-guzzling behemoths popular in North America were not attractive in Europe, where city streets are narrow and petrol prices are sky-high. Nor could Britain's left-hand automobiles come to America without alterations.

Still, there were many signs that product universality was on the way. One needed only observe the large and once fragmented U.S. market to appreciate that geographic diversity was giving way to homogeneity with each passing year. Krispy Kreme donut shops, once icons of Southern living, appeared in Boston, Las Vegas, and Honolulu. Seattle's Starbucks quickly spread to three thousand locations across the country. The Home Depot and Wal-Mart stores were cropping up everywhere. Many regional and local brands had already succumbed to national brands. It seemed logical that this trend would extend to the global stage.

Thus far (and to the relief of many consumers), this homogenization has made much less progress than Levitt anticipated. Reflecting on Levitt's thesis twenty years later, Harvard marketing professor John Quelch postulated that a global economic slump and anti-American sentiment had put a damper (temporarily) on the move toward global brands.[2] This lack of progress, if that's the right phrase, should caution marketing managers as they make product decisions. Will buyers in foreign markets respond favorably to the same products, packaging, and promotion as do domestic customers? If not, to what extent must offerings be customized for foreign tastes and requirements?

The answers to these questions are found through market research—the same research that any manager would apply to domestic markets. Simply assuming that foreign customers will respond positively to an existing product could lead to costly failure. Author and scholar Philip Kotler provides some examples of these failures in his classic textbook.[3] Consider these examples:

> *Coca-Cola had to withdraw its two-liter bottle in Spain after discovering that few Spaniards owned refrigerators with large enough compartments to accommodate it.*
>
> *General Foods squandered millions trying to introduce packaged cake mixes to Japanese consumers. The company failed to note that only 3 percent of Japanese homes were equipped with ovens.*
>
> *General Foods' Tang initially failed in France because it was positioned as a substitute for orange juice at breakfast. The French drink little orange juice and almost none at breakfast.*

The features, performance, and physical characteristics of a product that is successful in one market may or may not have to be altered to ensure its success in another. For example, European and Asian homes and rooms are generally smaller than those in America, and energy prices are much higher. This means that kitchen and laundry appliances must be more compact and energy efficient.

Products in many categories, however, can be distributed worldwide without problems. These include many industrial products and consumer products that target young buyers. The youth market, more than other consumer segments, is very accepting of global products if they are "the latest thing" and "cool." Swatch watches, cell phones, and Sony's PlayStation fit this description. Products used outside the home tend to be less culture-bound.[4]

## Efficiency Versus Market Suitability

You face a difficult trade-off with respect to products. On the one hand, pushing a standard product in all markets results in cost efficiencies because of economies of scale. On the other hand, a standard product may not sell well because of geographic differences in needs, tastes, and safety regulations. Thus, you must find a balance between the efficiencies of standardization and the greater market acceptance that comes from adapting products to local tastes, as shown in figure 12-1. Fundamentally, this trade-off is no different from the one you face in trying to satisfy different segments in domestic markets.

FIGURE 12-1

**The product trade-off**

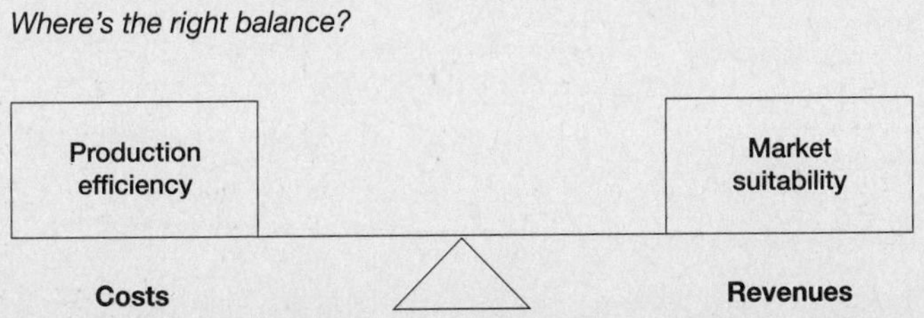

*Where's the right balance?*

Production efficiency        Market suitability

Costs        Revenues

It's the old trade-off of mass production and customization, this time played in a different arena.

## The Global Product Platform

One way around the trade-off between efficiency and market suitability is to design a global product platform that can be altered inexpensively to accommodate the requirements of different national markets.

The global steam iron designed by Sunbeam and its then international affiliate, Rowenta, provides an early example. In this case, engineers, marketers, and executives of the two companies were brought together to review market research and to study the products of key competitors. Two committees were created: a marketing committee and a technical committee. The former was charged with determining the feature set required by customers in different markets; the latter's job was to create a design capable of providing those features and satisfying regulatory standards in all national markets. That design would have to establish the product as the low-cost leader. The technical committee had to develop a set of specifications capable of satisfying electrical safety codes in all major markets.

The final platform design, when compared with Sunbeam's existing steam iron, made major reductions in parts (46 percent) and fasteners (84 percent). Its elements were so modular that the company could manufacture a wide variety of derivative irons from the same platform while still retaining a cost advantage. The design enabled good, better, and best versions capable of meeting the unique needs of different segments within regional markets.

The Sunbeam Global Iron was introduced in 1986 and immediately boosted the company's annual iron sales by 3.7 times.[5]


Take a moment to think about your company's products and services. How well do they conform to customer preferences and requirements in foreign markets? Have you used market research to answer that question? Some product issues can be solved with packaging and positioning, but others must be addressed through product design. Which applies to your situation?

## Promotion

Promotion covers all communications with current and potential customers: advertising, branding efforts, introductory coupons, and positioning. In most cases, promotion needs more customizing than do the other elements of the marketing mix. It touches the perceptions and psyches of customers, which are closely linked with culture, traditions, and social expectations.

Thus, a Western cosmetics maker cannot produce a TV commercial showing a scantily clad woman applying makeup and run it in parts of the Islamic world, where it would be viewed as scandalous. So, here again, you are faced with a trade-off between the cost efficiencies of standardized promotional materials and more costly, but more effective, customized versions.

Some companies have gotten around this trade-off by producing ads having universal appeal. A prime example is Coca-Cola's "I'd like to teach the world to sing" commercial, first launched in 1971. This ad, shot on an Italian hilltop, featured five hundred young people of all races and many nationalities, dressed in their traditional garb, standing hand in hand and raising their voices in a song of worldwide fraternity. It conjured an appealing picture of global peace, harmony, and youthful optimism during a time of war and social unrest—and, of course, it associated these universally appealing themes with Coca-Cola. The ad was a huge success. The song itself was so popular that a non-Coca-Cola version was produced, featuring a popular singing group of the time, and released in many languages. Both the recording and its sheet music were huge hits.[6]

Qantas, an Australian airline company, did something similar in the years that followed. It developed a lavishly filmed television commercial showing a chorus of children set against a background of iconic landmarks associated with the many destinations served by Qantas. It was attractive, uplifting, and in conformance with universal cultural values. After it was in the can, the original English voice-over could be altered to suit other markets.

Which approach to promotion is most suited to your products, goals, and overseas markets? The cheapest approach is to spin off your existing media ads, simply substituting the local language. Alternatively, you can adapt the same ads to suit specific markets. Or you could go for universality from the very start. Each approach is bound to produce a different impact.

## Place (or Distribution)

Distribution can be the most vexing aspect of global marketing. A product must make its way from the producer to the final buyer by means of one or more channels. The simplest approach is to sell your goods to a trading company, which assumes the responsibility for pushing them onward to customers abroad. But that arrangement takes control out of your hands.

The least simple approach, but the one with the greatest control, is to set up your own distribution network in the target country, using an in-country subsidiary staffed by locals who know the language and understand the market and business culture (see figure 12-2). Creating and managing such an arrangement require substantial investments of capital and management energy.

Somewhere between these extremes are these options:

- A joint venture formed with a successful independent company

- Company sales agents located in the target market

- Independent sales agents located in the target market

The right choice among these options is usually the consequence of your goals and expectations as well as the company's size. In many instances you will move through these options as you build foreign sales and gain confidence in your ability to manage and market abroad.

**FIGURE 12-2**

**Typical distribution options**

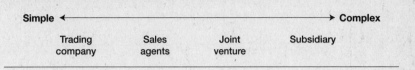

For example, a German manufacturer of electric components might begin by hiring a South Korean national to represent its products to original equipment makers (OEMs) in that country. As the volume of sales increases, the German company might see the wisdom of creating a South Korean subsidiary to sell its German-made goods and to design, manufacture, and sell components that meet the exact specifications of Korean OEMs.

# Price

What should you charge for your product in newly targeted foreign markets? Pricing in global markets is complex because of many factors. Aside from regulations that forbid *dumping*—the pricing of goods at less than their cost of production or less than the price at which they are normally offered in their countries of origin—producers are generally free to charge whatever they want. An Italian maker of bicycle components might, for example, sell its top-end sprockets to a New Zealand bike maker for 80 euros, and to a Finnish firm for 70 euros. Customers, of course, are equally free not to buy them at those prices.

On the one hand, exporters are justified in charging more to recoup the costs of tariffs and transportation. But in the end, what the market will bear is the ultimate determinant of what the price should be. There is no inherent right to any particular profit margin.

As long as antidump rules are observed, you are free to follow whatever pricing strategy will further your goals—as in the domestic market. Thus, you can price low, accepting a reduced margin in the hope of capturing market share. Or you can price high if customers perceive the product to be unique, exotic, or superior.

One of the pitfalls of differential pricing is that it can create arbitrage situations that can undermine your distribution arrangements. These are generally called gray markets. Consider this hypothetical example:

> *Gizmo Ceramics, a British firm, has distributors in the United States and Mexico and sells its product in each country for $100 per case. To meet its high labor and operating costs, the U.S. distributor must resell the product to local retailers at $175 per case, whereas the Mexican distributor has been prospering by selling the same items to Mexican retailers for $125 per case—a difference of $50. (Note: U.S. dollars are used in this example to avoid confusion.) A number of U.S. retailers of Gizmo products figure this out and begin placing all their orders with the Mexican distributor, saving $50 on each case, minus the incremental shipping cost. Soon, the U.S. distributor goes out of business, upsetting Gizmo's distribution scheme.*

Theoretically, there is nothing wrong with a gray market when the losers add no value to justify their higher prices. Economists would even say that the gray market creates more efficiency. However, producers need order and discipline in their distribution networks and usually take action to enforce it. There are different enforcement methods: policing of distribution agreements; cutting back supply to gray market distributors in the low-priced countries; and altering the design of products shipped to different countries. Policing of gray markets will only get more difficult as the Internet makes it possible for buyers to see and take advantage of low prices wherever they may be found.

## Controlling Global Marketing Decisions

Every marketing plan reflects dozens of decisions you've made about product, pricing, place, and promotion. When the plan involves marketing across borders, you must consider an added twist. Where should those decisions be made—at the home office, or within the markets being served?

This question becomes more pertinent as you put boots on the ground in the foreign market—a sales office, a joint venture company, or a subsidiary. Who, for example, should determine design, packaging, and naming of the product—the people back in Cleveland, or the subsidiary operating out of Madrid? Who should commission and approve media advertising? The price of your product?

There are, of course, no absolutely right or wrong answers to these questions. In the end, they depend on the situation, your approach to centralization versus decentralization, and your experience in overseas markets. Some companies have headquarters-based product-line managers who make all decisions, foreign and domestic, for their lines. This approach enhances the ability to leverage corporatewide assets, but perhaps at the cost of losing the tacit knowledge that only people closer to their markets can have.

Philip Kotler describes three strategies for organizing the cross-border effort and its many decisions:[7]

- **Global.** This approach treats the entire world as a single market. Of necessity it emphasizes a standard approach to product and marketing, with centralized decision making. As Kotler puts it, "This strategy is warranted when the forces for global integration are strong and the forces for national responsiveness are weak."

- **Multinational.** Here, the world is seen as a portfolio of national opportunities. Companies that follow this strategy move more decision-making authority to their nation-based organizations.

- **"Glocal."** This strategy is based on standardized platforms that are adapted to local requirements. Companies that adopt this strategy are more likely to organize around business units than around headquarters or national units.

Is your company currently selling abroad? If it is, take a look at figure 12-3. Note where decisions for the listed issues are made: at the

FIGURE 12-3

## The locus of control

|  | Home Control | Local Control |
|---|---|---|
| **Product** | | |
| R&D | | |
| Manufacturing | | |
| Material sourcing | | |
| Packaging decisions | | |
| Product-line management | | |
| **Pricing** | | |
| **Promotion** | | |
| Brand development | | |
| Advertising | | |
| Sales | | |
| **Distribution** | | |

*Source:* John A. Quelch and Edward J. Hoff, "Customizing Global Marketing," *Harvard Business Review*, May–June 1986. Adapted with permission.

home office or within the market affected by those decisions. Now ask yourself, Are these the best places to control decisions?

## Summing Up

- On the product front, companies that cross borders face a choice between trying to push existing products or adapting them to the unique requirements of foreign markets: efficiency versus suitability.

- Global product platforms represent a potential solution to the efficiency versus suitability problem.

- In most cases, promotion needs more customizing than do other elements of the marketing mix.

- Distribution arrangements are often the most vexing aspect of global marketing. The simplest approach is to deal through a trading company; the most complex is to set up a distribution subsidiary in a country or region.

- Transportation costs and tariffs often result in products being priced differently in different national markets. This can create gray markets.

- Companies that market across borders must determine where decisions on pricing, product design, distribution, and promotion will be made.

# The Future of Marketing

*Tomorrow's Challenges*

## Key Topics Covered in This Chapter

- *The end of information asymmetry*

- *Delivering on marketing promises*

- *Cutting through the marketing clutter*

- *Growing fragmentation in U.S. consumer markets*

- *Accountability for results*

- *Ethical marketing behavior*

E VERY BUSINESS discipline faces important challenges. This chapter looks at six challenges that marketers must grapple with now and in the years ahead.

## Today's Buyers Have More Information

Marketers and the organizations that employ them face a number of challenges as they look toward the future. For one thing, the developed economies of the world have excess supply and production capacity in many product and service categories. The automobile industry is a prime example of this overcapacity on the manufacturing front, and some observers believe that the square footage devoted to consumer retail is in the same situation. The emergence of manufacturing competitors from once dormant parts of the globe has exacerbated this supply and demand problem and has forced domestic producers to fight ever harder for market share.

The Internet has also made the life of some marketers more difficult. True, as chapter 11 pointed out, the Internet has opened a new channel through which everything from books to accredited college courses to marketing messages can be sent with remarkable efficiency (if not assured profitability). But the Internet has also shifted a great deal of power into the hands of consumers and business buyers.

In the past, a significant asymmetry of information favored sellers. Sellers knew from competitor research which rivals had the lowest prices and which ones offered which features and warranties. Most buyers had much less information, and getting it was difficult and time-consuming. Buyers had to rely on sellers—a biased source—for the information they needed to make purchase decisions.

The Web changed this situation by making it easier for consumers to gain information about products and prices. Today, a person interested in buying a top-end digital camera can easily find product reviews, user ratings, and expert ratings via Yahoo! and similar sites. If a Nikon D-70 is what he wants, one click will display a long list of seller prices from around the country. Customer reviews of these sellers indicate which are most helpful and reliable. The buyer can get the best price and the level of service he demands—and all in a few minutes. This new information balance has shifted substantial power to consumers and will likely lead to thinner margins as each vendor tries to be the most attractive one on the list.

How marketers will respond to this new balance of information is unclear. Perhaps the best approach they can take is to work harder at differentiating their products and services and making them better than anything the competition offers. Success in this effort will put a seller in a class of its own.

## Delivering on the Promise

Marketers make promises. "Unbeatable prices." "Unmatched performance." "Say goodbye to unwanted pounds." "We'll treat you right." One of the challenges for companies is to deliver on those promises.

The record shows, at least in the United States, that there is a long way to go. According to the American Customer Satisfaction Index as of year-end 2004, consumers were slightly less satisfied with products and services than they were ten years ago, when the index was first compiled. Fourth-quarter results registered the largest quarterly drop in seven years. Does this reflect a failure of business to deliver, or rising expectations among the buying public? No matter which it is, one challenge of the future will be to close the gap between the rhetoric of what companies and their brands stand for and the reality experienced by customers.

How can this gap be closed? We recommend that companies spend more time studying their customers and finding out what they value most—and not what fascinates marketers and product developers. In most cases, what customers value most is a product that is uncomplicated and performs as described. This means that developers would do well to design products and services that provide value with a minimum of unnecessary bells and whistles; and it means that marketers must rein in their claims and avoid raising unrealistic expectations.

Delivering on promises also relates to marketing budgets. CEOs are getting tighter with marketing budgets. The reason is no secret: they cannot see a clear payoff for all the money spent on marketing. In some cases CEOs' instincts on this matter are right; they are not getting an adequate return on their investments. In many others, however, the return on marketing investments is anyone's guess because of a failure to track performance. The burden is on marketing managers to track and report the effectiveness of their programs and expenditures, something that is easier said than done. More on this later.

## Cutting Through the Clutter

Consumers are barraged by marketing messages wherever they turn. Pop-ups and banners on Web pages. TV and radio spots every few minutes. A daily dose of direct mail catalogs. Billboards. Telephone calls from telemarketers and stockbrokers. Clothing logos. Infomercials disguised as legitimate programming. Commercial messages in movie theatres. Marketing guru Seth Godin refers to this practice as "interruption marketing." Whatever you're doing, some advertiser interrupts and expects you to pay attention.

Consumers aren't pleased by interruptions and they are tuning them out, if not fighting back. They reflexively toss out unsolicited catalogs and junk mail unopened. They leave the room or surf to other channels when commercials punctuate the evening news. And they hang up on telemarketers. Between October 2003 and October 2004, 57 percent of the U.S. adult population listed their telephone numbers with the National "Do Not Call" Registry. Others are recording their favorite TV programs and then skipping the ads as they view them. As a result of consumer resistance, marketing messages costing billions of dollars are being tuned out, tossed out, avoided, and ignored.

The challenge for marketers is to cut through the clutter and get noticed. And once again, success begins with a solid understanding of customers. Customers are not put off by messages about things that interest them. For example, people who are active in the stock market don't mind taking an occasional cold call from a stockbroker; they figure they might learn something of value. College professors must keep up with the latest textbooks in their disciplines, so they routinely welcome visits by publishers' reps to their offices. Those salespeople provide useful information and usually follow up with complimentary copies of books that professors can use. Similarly, millions of Internet users voluntarily sign up for e-mails from vendors whose products and services they value.

Intuit—seller of TurboTax, a software product used by millions of U.S. taxpayers in preparing their returns—is a good example of how to gain customer attention by providing something useful to customers. Each issue of its TurboTax e-newsletter contains useful information: updates on tax laws, advice on how to avoid an audit, overlooked deductions, and so forth. Of course, Intuit manages to get lots of plugs for its products into this newsletter, but it's doubtful that many recipients resent that because (1) they volunteered to receive it, (2) they received something of real value along with it, and (3) they can unsubscribe without a hitch.

So the secret to cutting through the clutter is not to scream louder or interrupt customers more often than your rivals. Rather, the secret is to package your message with something that customers value.

## Market Fragmentation

Thirty years ago, most people in the United States could be reliably reached through the three major national TV networks (ABC, CBS, and NBC). This is no longer the case. The country's pet lovers are watching Animal Planet, Hispanics are tuned to Spanish language stations, sports fans are glued to ESPN, and collectors are over on PBS, watching Antiques Roadshow. At the same time, political conservatives have switched their radio dials to Sean Hannity's or Rush Limbaugh's show, while the evangelicals have surfed over to the Liberty Channel network to hear Rev. Jerry Falwell's TV homilies. Meanwhile, many American Jews are reading their daily copy of *Forward,* and political liberals are tuning in to Air America.

Some social observers warn that the United States runs the risk of becoming Balkanized by ethnic affiliations, language, and politics. And this warning has merit. The country now has so-called red states (conservative) and blue states (liberal), European Americans, white Southerners, African Americans, Hispanic Americans, Afro-Caribbean Americans, and other hyphenated groups. Add to these groups trade unionists, environmentalists, gays and lesbians (soon to have their own cable TV channel), and, of course, the Red Sox Nation. One wonders whether the national motto, *E pluribus unum* ("Out of many, one"), will be shortened to *pluribus.* Because of large-scale immigration, European countries face a similar phenomenon.

This tendency of people to cluster into groups presents marketers with a serious challenge. On the one hand, people's separation into market segments with strong ethnic, income, geographic, behavioral, or affinity characteristics has made it easier to develop products and services to address their needs and tastes. On the other hand, segmentation fragments the total market into niches that are often too small for organizations to serve profitably—at least for large companies that depend on economies of scale and national advertising. For small, nimble companies, fragmentation may represent a distinct opportunity, because it neutralizes the strengths of large rivals.

Reaching and selling to these small segments will continue to vex marketers in the years ahead.

## Measurement and Accountability

Every business and every business function must set goals, work toward achieving them, and then measure the results. Marketing is good at the first two but falls short on the third. So it is not surprising that CEOs are getting stingy with marketing spending. The manufacturing people can demonstrate how investments in new equipment will cut labor costs and scrappage. The CTO can reasonably estimate the performance and cost improvements that go hand in hand with a new Web hosting arrangement. Better still, the actual return on those investments can be measured after implementation. But when the marketing VP proposes a media campaign, the CEO can only guess at the results.

Writing in the spring 1995 issue of *Business Strategy Review*, Patrick Barwise, a professor of marketing at the London Business School, identified marketing measurement and accountability as a subject that would receive greater emphasis in the years ahead. Speaking ten years later, Barwise cited incomplete progress in making marketing accountable for results. His assessment is supported by a recent study, which found that only 25 percent of companies surveyed measured the impact of marketing on their business goals.[1]

Technology can certainly help. Database marketers can measure response rates to direct mail and e-mail campaigns—and the revenues they produce. They can also use their technology to sort customers in terms of loyalty and profitability. The short-term benefits of price promotions can also be measured and tabulated, thanks to technology. This ability to measure costs and responses provides greater predictability to marketing investments. Predictability is important to decision makers.

Other data can be used to measure parts of the marketing effort, including the following:

- **Sales revenues.** This number measures sales force effectiveness, although it is difficult to separate from changes in product offerings, pricing changes, and other initiatives.

- **Brand awareness.** This indicates something about the effectiveness of a company's branding agency and media buys.

- **Customer satisfaction.** Aspects of the product, price, fulfillment, and after-sales service affect this measure, making it difficult to use in assessing performance.

The impact of media ads is less clear. The $2.4 million average price tag for a half-minute ad during the 2005 Super Bowl football game should be enough to make any executive say, "Show me the projected return—and how you determined it." Even at the paltry $400,000 charged for the same thirty seconds on a prime time network TV show, the CEO and CFO are bound to raise their eyebrows.

The knotty measurement problem has moved consultant Michael Fischler to write as follows:

> In my view, the true measure of marketing is this: How many profitable markets do we develop or strengthen for our new or existing products? Marketing is, in the end, about market development. Our job—in its "purest" sense—is to reach into the relevant business universes and discover new markets and segments our products and services can profitably penetrate, and new products that can profitably serve our markets and segments. If you agree with that, then measuring Marketing becomes concrete and objective—maybe, Lord help us, even easy. We can look at our enterprise, and with a simple matrix evaluate our markets and our segments. And we can then look at that same matrix a year from now (or at more frequent intervals if we like), and evaluate how many new markets and segments we've added or strengthened. If we track our efforts carefully, we can figure out what it cost us to do this, and what we're earning from them. And voilà! An objective, dollars-and-cents measurement of whether our marketing activities are providing value to the enterprise.
>
> If we dig into the market landscape, do our homework, and return to the conference table with the suggestion that Product A, based on a mix of quantifiable information and plain old instinct, can penetrate a new international marketplace, we've done our job. If we determine that Product B, properly repositioned, can reach a new demographic, we've done our job. If

*we determine that Industry C is ready for a new product that solves an as yet untended problem—and define that product—we've done our job. If we determine that Market D, properly cared for, can become more loyal through a careful retention strategy, we've done our job.[2]*

After marketing has done its job, says Fischler, it's time for the sales force, the ad agency, the product developers, customer fulfillment, and other players to do theirs—and take responsibility for their own metrics.

Measurement and accountability is one of marketing's biggest problems. How is it handled in your company? Are investments linked to measurable results? (Note: if you're looking for a way to start, begin with Philip Kotler's "Marketing Effectiveness Review Instrument," a self-diagnostic test of a company's standing in key areas: customer orientation, integrated marketing organization, adequate market information, strategic orientation, and operational effectiveness.)[3]

## The Ethics of Marketing

Ethics are standards of behavior that govern the conduct of individuals, groups, and business organizations. More than other functions of a business, marketing is a potential source of ethical problems. To appreciate why, think about some of the legitimate things that marketing must do and consider how they invite unethical behavior:

- **Create awareness.** Hammer people over and over with the message; invade their privacy if necessary.

- **Help the company's products and services stand out from the crowd.** Exaggerate the positives; conceal the negatives in the "fine print."

- **Motivate the customer to buy.** Overpromise.

Advertisers often run afoul of ethical standards, as seen by the public. How many TV ads have you seen in which automobiles are driven irresponsibly? "This baby has power to spare!" Would you want your family on the same highway with an eighteen-year-old boy who thinks these ads are cool? How many ads for banks and credit cards encourage liberal borrowing for personal consumption? "Go on, take that dream vacation. You deserve it. And our card makes it *so* easy." Never mind that a great many people are already up to their eyeballs in debt, and these are the people most likely to respond to the ads. In particular, advertising aimed at young children has provoked a great many complaints from the public over the years.

The pressure to be noticed by message-numbed consumers tempts advertisers to shout still louder and be more blatant in their appeals—even past the point of ethical behavior. At the same time, the Internet has opened new areas of concern, most notably the gathering and unauthorized use of customer information.

The most unethical marketing practices are eventually reformed through statutes that prohibit those practices and fine offenders—this is how "bait and switch" tactics, telemarketing, and phony promotional contests were dealt with in the United States. But statutes will never rein in the many bad behaviors committed in the name of marketing. Only sound ethics within companies and within industry and professional groups can do that. As Ethics Quality, Inc., has put it, "Ethics work like an oil filter in the marketing engine: they filter out the impurities so the oil can enable the engine to work. All firms need ethics to filter away the abrasive nature of competitive life so good people can target, attract and retain good customers for the firm."[4] That's good advice.

It's hard to know whether the public is more annoyed by marketing now than it was in the past, or whether people are simply more outspoken these days in their discontent. In any case, marketing does not enjoy a good reputation, and every revelation of unethical practices further tarnishes it. This unhappy situation surely reduces the return on marketing investments. Thus, one of the profession's challenges is to improve public confidence in marketing communications. The best way to accomplish that is to ensure that every promotion, every ad, every pricing arrangement, and every use of customer information conforms to a high ethical standard.

The challenges described in this chapter are substantial. Three of them—delivering on the promise, implementing measurement and accountability, and conforming to ethical behavior—are internal and under the control of company managers and employees. They can deal with these challenges if they take them seriously. The other challenges are external and less easily handled through direct action. A single company cannot, for example, change the fact that information has become more symmetrical. Nor can it eliminate the clutter of advertising and promotions that impedes marketing communications. Even these larger problems, however, can be overcome through sound strategy and creative marketing.

## Summing Up

- The asymmetry of information that has long favored sellers is coming to an end, in large part because of the Internet. Sellers must find ways to adjust to this new situation.

- Companies must deliver on their promises—that is, they must close the gap between the rhetoric of what they and their brands stand for and the reality experienced by customers.

- People are tuning out marketing messages. The remedy is to offer messages that contain something of value.

- The U.S. consumer market has fragmented into submarkets based on ethnicity, language, political affiliation, and so forth. Some of these smaller markets cannot be profitably served by large companies that depend on economies of scale.

- Marketing suffers from a failure to measure results in terms of strategy goals.

- Marketers, and advertisers in particular, often run afoul of ethical standards. The public's recognition of this behavior surely reduces the return on marketing investments.

# Useful Implementation Tools

This appendix contains three useful tools you can use to execute concepts described in this book. All were developed for our online publication, Harvard ManageMentor®.

1. **A Template for Your Marketing Plan (figure A–1).** This tool is an abbreviated version of a marketing plan that you can add to or adapt to fit your needs.

2. **Calculating the Value of a Customer (figure A–2).** Use this worksheet to think through what your customers value, which you can think of as an equation. The service value as determined by the customer is equal to the results received multiplied by how the service is delivered, in relation to the price of the service multiplied by any costs for acquiring the service. The values in the equation are relative, because different customers often want different things, or the same customer may want different things at different times. For example, in one situation customers may place more value on convenience and the opportunity to save time, and in another situation they may place more value on price. Think through how you can leverage the factors in this equation to add value for the customer and enhance your business.

3. **Calculating the Lifetime Value of a Customer (figure A–3).** Use this worksheet to calculate the lifetime value of one of your customers. Go to www.elearning.hbsp.org/businesstools for an interactive version that will calculate your entries.

**FIGURE A-1**

## A template for your marketing plan

---

### Marketing plan

Product name: _____

Date of plan: _____        Fiscal year: _____

Marketing manager(s): _____        Contact information: _____

_____

Contributors to the plan: _____        Contact information: _____

_____

Approved by: _____        Approval date: _____

---

**Market review**

**List key market factors**  *(Describe the market in terms of size, growth, segments, geographic factors, and so forth.)*

**Describe the industry climate and significant new trends**  *(For example, what is the current economic condition of this industry? What new trends are emerging?)*

**Competitive environment**

| | Key competitors | Market share | Offering/price |
|---|---|---|---|
| 1. | _____ | _____ | _____ |
| 2. | _____ | _____ | _____ |
| 3. | _____ | _____ | _____ |
| 4. | _____ | _____ | _____ |

---

**The product**

**Prior year revenue, actual versus forecast**

**This year revenue forecast**  *(by distribution channel, if indicated)*

**Product status**

❑ **New product?**        ❑ **Enhanced product?**        **Launch date:** _____

| | Features | Benefits |
|---|---|---|
| 1. | _____ | _____ |
| 2. | _____ | _____ |
| 3. | _____ | _____ |
| 4. | _____ | _____ |

**Product positioning** *(Note if prior positioning was effective or needs to be reconsidered.)*

---

**Product differentiator, unique selling point, or competitive advantage**

---

**The customer**

**Relevant customer or user demographics** *(What is the typical user profile? Where are users located and how do you reach them?)*

**Buyer behavior** *(Why do people buy your product? What needs does it meet? Is it a planned or impulse purchase? How does price figure into their purchase?)*

---

**Distribution channels**

---

**Market research plan or usability testing**

|  | What | When | Result |
|---|---|---|---|
| Prior | _____ | _____ | _____ |
| Planned | _____ | _____ | _____ |

---

**Opportunity analysis** *(See also the SWOT tool)*

*Based upon an analysis of the product or service's inherent strengths, weaknesses, external opportunities, and threats, what are the major opportunities and issues facing the product and/or brand?*

---

**Financial objectives**

---

**Marketing objectives**

*Continued*

| Marketing strategy | | |
|---|---|---|
| | | |

| Marketing tactics or action programs | | |
|---|---|---|
| **Program** | **Scheduled dates** | **Estimated cost** |
| Advertising/media | | |
| Merchandising | | |
| Publicity | | |
| Trade shows/exhibits | | |
| Web marketing | | |
| Promotions | | |
| Endorsements | | |
| Sales incentives | | |
| Sales support materials | | |
| Dealer incentives or terms | | |
| Special offers | | |
| Up-sell/cross-sell | | |
| Pricing strategy | | |
| Others | | |
| **Measures of success** | | |
| *(Specify the expected results that signal success; for example, a 3 percent click-through rate on an e-mail campaign.)* | | |
| **Projected profit and loss** | | |
| *(See also the Pro Forma tool in Harvard ManageMentor® Finance Essentials topic.)* | | |
| **Revenues** | **Costs** | **Margin** |
| | | |
| | | |
| | | |
| **Controls** | | |
| *(For example, when will progress toward goals be reviewed and by whom? Is there a contingency plan if actual results deviate from projections?)* | | |

*Source:* Harvard ManageMentor® on Marketing Essentials, adapted with permission.

FIGURE A-2

## Calculating the value of a customer

| Customer value equation worksheet | |
|---|---|
| **What customers value** | |
| *Fill in this equation with descriptions of what your customers value. You do not have to use a specific dollar amount in the price category, but you can use descriptive terms such as high, low, competitive pricing, everyday low price (EDLP), premium, discounted, and so forth.* | |
| **Results** | **Delivery/process quality** |
| What results do your customers want? | How do they want the results delivered? |
| | X | |
| *Look at the above in relationship to the factors below.* | |
| **Price** | **Access costs** |
| What price are they willing to pay for the product or service? | What costs are they willing to incur to get the product or service? |
| | X | |
| **Value summary** | |
| What are the key customer value equations most prevalent in your business? | |
| What factors or situations could affect these equations? What ones can you alter or control? | |
| How can you leverage these factors to increase the value of your service (or product) to the customer? *For example, increase convenience while keeping price the same.* | |

*Source:* Harvard ManageMentor® on Marketing Essentials, adapted with permission.

**FIGURE A-3**

## Calculating the lifetime value of a customer

| Customer name |
|---|

| Basic formula |
|---|

| Estimate number of customer transactions in lifetime | Number of purchases per visit | Average price per purchase ($) | Cost to acquire a customer ($) | Lifetime value of a customer ($) |
|---|---|---|---|---|
| 0    X | 0    X | $ 0.00    – | $ 0.00    = | $ 0.00 |

**Projected formula, five-year period**

| | Revenue (Include gross revenue generated) | Cost (Calculate costs to service this customer, including marketing, and costs of making and delivering product or service) | Referrals (Add net value of referred accounts) | Profit ($) |
|---|---|---|---|---|
| Year 1 | $ 0.00   – | $ 0.00   + | $ 0.00   = | $ |
| Year 2 | $ 0.00   – | $ 0.00   + | $ 0.00   = | $ |
| Year 3 | $ 0.00   – | $ 0.00   + | $ 0.00   = | $ |
| Year 4 | $ 0.00   – | $ 0.00   + | $ 0.00   = | $ |
| Year 5 | $ 0.00   – | $ 0.00   + | $ 0.00   = | $ |
| | | | Total | $ |

Source: Harvard ManageMentor® on Marketing Essentials, adapted with permission.

# *Notes*

## Chapter 1

1. Alfred P. Sloan Jr., "Quarterly Dividend Mailing to GM Common Stockholders," General Motors Corporation, September 11, 1933. For a more complete look at the contents of this letter and Sloan's strikingly modern view, see Vincent P. Barabba, *Meeting of the Minds* (Boston: Harvard Business School Press, 1995), 12.

2. Peter F. Drucker, *Management: Tasks, Responsibilities, Practices* (New York: Harper & Row, 1974), 61.

3. Vincent P. Barabba, *Meeting of the Minds* (Boston: Harvard Business School Press, 1995), 2.

## Chapter 2

1. Carl von Clausewitz, *On War,* volume 1 (London: Kegan Paul, 1911), 177.

2. Edward Mead Earle, ed., *Makers of Modern Strategy* (Princeton, NJ: Princeton University Press, 1943).

3. Michael E. Porter, *Competitive Strategy* (New York: Free Press, 1985), xxiv.

4. Michael E. Porter, "What Is Strategy?" *Harvard Business Review*, November–December 1996, 61–78.

## Chapter 3

1. Vincent P. Barabba and Gerald Zaltman, *Hearing the Voice of the Market* (Boston: Harvard Business School Press, 1991), 61.

2. Vincent P. Barabba, *Meeting of the Minds* (Boston: Harvard Business School Press, 1995), 127.

3. Dorothy Leonard and Jeffrey F. Rayport, "Spark Innovation Through Empathetic Design," *Harvard Business Review*, November–December 1997, 102–113.

4. Patrick Barwise and Seán Meehan, *Simply Better* (Boston: Harvard Business School Press, 2004), 66–67.

## Chapter 4

1. B. Joseph Pine II, *Mass Customization* (Boston: Harvard Business School Press, 1993), xiii.

2. Philip Kotler, *Marketing Management,* millennium edition (Upper Saddle River, NJ: Prentice Hall, 2000), 274.

3. Al Ries and Jack Trout, *The 22 Immutable Laws of Marketing* (New York: HarperBusiness, 1993), 35.

## Chapter 5

1. George Day and David J. Reibstein, *Wharton on Dynamic Competitive Strategy* (New York: John Wiley & Sons, 1997), 23.

2. Michael E. Porter, "How Competitive Forces Shape Strategy," *Harvard Business Review*, March–April 1979, 113–135.

3. Ibid.

## Chapter 6

1. David Bovet and Joseph Martha, *Value Nets* (New York: John Wiley & Sons, 2000), 30.

2. Patrick Barwise and Seán Meehan, *Simply Better* (Boston: Harvard Business School Press, 2004), 20.

## Chapter 7

1. Eric Almquist, Andy Pierce, and César Paiva, "Customer Value Growth: Keeping Ahead of the Active Customer," *Mercer Management Journal*, 13 June 2002.

2. Robert E. Wayland and Paul M. Cole, *Customer Connections* (Boston: Harvard Business School Press, 1997), 103.

3. Frederick Reichheld and W. Earl Sasser Jr., "Zero Defections: Quality Comes to Services," *Harvard Business Review*, September–October 1990, 110.

4. Frederick Reichheld, *The Loyalty Effect* (Boston: Harvard Business School Press, 1996), 52.

### Chapter 8

1. Anthony W. Ulwick, "Turn Customer Input into Innovation," *Harvard Business Review*, January 2003, 91–97.

2. Marc H. Meyer and Alvin P. Lehnerd, *The Power of Product Platforms* (New York: The Free Press, 1997), xii.

3. Ibid., 5–15.

4. Booz Allen & Hamilton, Inc., "New Product Management for the 1980s," Booz Allen & Hamilton, Inc., 1982.

5. Robert G. Cooper, "Stage-Gate Systems: A New Tool for Managing New Products," *Business Horizons,* May–June 1990, 45–54.

6. Vincent P. Barabba, *Meeting of the Minds* (Boston: Harvard Business School Press, 1995), 137.

7. Patrick Barwise and Seán Meehan, *Simply Better* (Boston: Harvard Business School Press, 2004), 94.

### Chapter 9

1. Robert J. Dolan, "Pricing: A Value-Based Approach," Note 9-500-071 (Boston: Harvard Business School, December 21, 1999), 89–90.

### Chapter 10

1. For a full discussion of the six M's, see Robert J. Dolan, "Integrated Marketing Communications," Note 9-599-087 (Boston: Harvard Business School, revised June 1, 2000).

### Chapter 11

1. Gerry McGovern, "Internet Marketing Motto: Be useful," MarketingProfs.com, December 7, 2004, www.marketingprofs.com/4/mcgovern32.asp.

2. "Market Forecast: U.S. Retail 2004–2008," Jupiter Research, January 2004, jupitermedia.com/corporate/releases/04.01.20-newjupresearch.html.

3. "Convicted Spammer Gets Nine-Year Sentence," *Wall Street Journal Online*, 8 April 2004.

## Chapter 12

1. Theodore Levitt, "The Globalization of Markets," *Harvard Business Review*, May–June 1983, 92–102.

2. John A. Quelch, "The Return of the Global Brand," *Harvard Business Review*, August 2003, 22–23.

3. Philip Kotler, *Marketing Management,* millennium edition (Upper Saddle River, NJ: Prentice Hall, 2000), 367.

4. John A. Quelch and Edward J. Hoff, "Customizing Global Marketing," *Harvard Business Review*, May–June 1986, 59–68.

5. The Sunbeam story was told to Richard Luecke by Alvin Lehnerd, a former Sunbeam executive, and later recounted in Marc H. Meyer and Alvin P. Lehnerd, *The Power of Product Platforms* (New York: Free Press, 1997), 105–117.

6. The full story of this ad—one of the most successful in history—is nicely told at www2.coca-cola.com/heritage/cokelore_hilltop_include.html.

7. Kotler, *Marketing Management,* 387–388.

## Chapter 13

1. As cited in Laura Patterson, "The Four Marketing Practices of Winners," MarketingProfs.com, March 8, 2005, marketingprofs.com/5/patterson3.asp.

2. Michael Fischler, "Fresh Focus," a biweekly e-newsletter of Markitek, markitek.com/archives.htm.

3. Philip Kotler, *Marketing Management,* millennium edition (Upper Saddle River, NJ: Prentice Hall, 2000), 707–708.

4. Ethics Quality, Inc., "Ethics and Culture Management Are Good for Business," ethicsquality.com/marketing.htm.

# Glossary

**ATMOSPHERICS**  The physical or psychological environment in which business is conducted. Atmospherics can be a powerful differentiator when customers expect a pleasant or interesting place in which to purchase items.

**BAIT AND HOOK**  A pricing strategy that sets the initial purchase price low but charges agressively for replacement parts or for other materials consumed in using the product. The razor blade is a familiar example.

**BRAND**  A name, term, sign, symbol, or design—or any combination of these—that identifies a product or service.

**BRAND EQUITY**  The financial value of a brand to a firm.

**BRAND EXTENSION**  The act of attaching a successful brand name to another product or service.

**BRANDING**  The communication effort that aims to help customers differentiate a product or service from that of rivals—and to view it in a favorable way.

**BREAKTHROUGH PRODUCT**  A product (or service) that brings one or more of the following to the market: an entirely new set of performance features—the product is new to the world; improvements in performance features that are many times greater; a sizable reduction in cost for the same features offered by other products. Breakthrough products change the basis of competition in their industry.

**COMMODITY**  An undifferentiated product or service.

**COMPETITOR**  From a business marketing viewpoint, a company that satisfies—or intends to satisfy—the same customer needs that your firm satisfies.

**CONJOINT ANALYSIS** A statistical technique for predicting how buyers will make trade-offs between attributes of an offer. Its objective is to determine what combination of a limited number of relevant attributes is most preferred by potential buyers. Market researchers find conjoint analysis useful in forecasting customer acceptance of new products and services.

**CUSTOMER DEVELOPMENT** Marketing activities that aim to expand the amount of profitable business conducted with current customers. Many refer to this activity as expanding one's "share of the wallet."

**DIFFERENTIATION** The act of setting a company's offers apart from those of competitors in meaningful ways.

**DUMPING** The practice of pricing goods at less than their cost of production, or less than the price at which they are offered in their countries of origin, for the purpose of entering a market or driving out competition.

**EMPATHETIC DESIGN** An idea-generating technique whereby researchers observe how people use existing products and services in their own environments. For example, a researcher may arrange to live in the home of a typical family to understand how they use an appliance to do regular chores.

**EXPERIENCE CURVE** A concept that holds that the cost of doing a repetitive task decreases by some percentage each time the cumulative volume of production doubles. A company that gets onto the experience curve sooner than an imitator can theoretically maintain a cost advantage.

**FOCUS GROUP** A small group of invited individuals who, guided by a trained moderator, discuss a product, service, their perceptions of a particular company, or even political issues.

**FOUR P'S OF MARKETING.** *See* Marketing mix.

**HORIZONTAL PRODUCT LINE** A product line that uses different product versions or configurations to appeal to different customer tastes.

**INCREMENTAL PRODUCT** A new product that exploits existing forms or technologies, either improving on something that exists or reconfiguring an existing form or technology to serve some other purpose.

**INTEGRATED MARKETING COMMUNICATIONS (IMC)** A strategic process for producing a consistent brand message at each customer touch point.

Its goal is to use multiple modes of communication in consistent, complementary ways to foster awareness of a company's products or services, inform people about features and benefits, and move them to make a purchase.

**INTERNET MARKETING**   Any activity that uses the Internet to advertise and sell goods and services to consumers, businesses, nonprofit institutions, or government.

**LEAD USERS**   Companies and individuals—customers and noncustomers— whose needs are far ahead of market trends. Existing products fail to meet their needs.

**MARKET CHANNELS**   Intermediary companies between producers and final consumers that make products or services available to consumers. Also called *trade channels* or *distribution channels*. Examples include retail stores, direct mail, and online sales.

**MARKET ORIENTATION**   A business orientation that holds that a company should understand what customers want, need, and value and then organize itself to produce and deliver the products and services customers truly value.

**MARKET-ORIENTED STRATEGIC PLANNING**   The managerial process of developing and maintaining a viable fit among a company's objectives, skills, and resources and its changing market opportunities.

**MARKET PLAN**   A tactical plan that lays out a campaign aimed at fulfilling the marketing strategy of a company. It indicates the timing of sales and promotional activities, pricing intentions, and distribution efforts. How the plan will be controlled and the results measured are also part of the plan.

**MARKET RESEARCH**   The formal collection, analysis, and reporting of external data that a company finds relevant to its businesses.

**MARKETING**   The process of planning and executing the conception, pricing, promotion, and distribution of ideas, goods, and services to create exchanges that satisfy individual and organizational goals.

**MARKETING CONCEPT**   The belief that a company can achieve its goals primarily by being more effective than its competitors at creating, delivering, and communicating value to its target markets. The marketing concept rests on four pillars: (1) identifying a target market, (2) focusing on customer needs, (3) coordinating all marketing functions from the customer's point of view, and (4) achieving profitability.

**MARKETING MIX**   The set of tools—product, price, place, and promotion—that a company uses to pursue its marketing objectives in the target market. Also called the "four P's" of marketing.

**MARKETING NETWORK**   A web of connections among a company and its supporting stakeholders—customers, employees, suppliers, distributors, and others—with whom it has built profitable business relationships. Companies that have the best marketing networks also have a major competitive edge.

**MASS CUSTOMIZATION**   A production approach that uses flexible manufacturing or modular design (or both) to produce goods that meet the unique needs of specific customers.

**NEED**   A basic human requirement, such as food, air, water, clothing, and shelter, as well as recreation, education, and entertainment.

**OPT IN**   In Web commerce, the act of volunteering one's name and e-mail address to receive free e-mail or a free newsletter from a vendor.

**PENETRATION PRICING**   A strategy that sets the initial price of the product (or service) lower than supply and demand conditions would dictate. Companies that adopt this strategy do so with the expectation that their product will be more widely accepted by the market: people who otherwise would not buy will buy, or people who are loyal to an estabished rival product will come over to their side.

**PLACE**   As an element of the marketing mix, place refers to the point of sale and distribution of the product or service. Place might refer to a retail store, a national distribution network, an e-commerce Web site, or a direct mail catalog.

**POSITIONING**   An attempt to manage the way potential customers perceive a product or service. Positioning articulates the central benefit of a market offering in the minds of target buyers.

**PRESTIGE PRICING**   A strategy that aims to create a perception of brand quality or exclusivity in the minds of customers by setting a high price.

**PRICE**   What a buyer must give up in exchange for a product. One of the elements of the marketing mix.

**PRICE ELASTICITY OF DEMAND**   A quantitative measure of customer price sensitivity.

**PRICE PROMOTION**   A collection of incentive tools, usually short term, designed to stimulate consumers to try a product or service, to buy it quickly, or to purchase more of it.

**PRICE SKIMMING**   A strategy through which the producer of a uniquely new item obtains high profits from buyers for whom the new product is a must-have item. Once profits have been skimmed from that segment of the market, the producer drops the price and skims the next tier of interested customers.

**PROCUREMENT**   The process by which a business buys materials or services from another business, with which it then creates products or services for its own customers.

**PRODUCT**   As an element of the marketing mix, product refers to the item (or service) offered to customers along with the intangibles that surround it: warranties, after-sales service, options, and so forth. The product is any offering that can satisfy a customer's need or want.

**PRODUCT CONCEPT**   The belief that consumers favor products that offer the highest quality, greatest performance, or innovative features.

**PRODUCT PLATFORM**   A set of subsystems and interfaces that forms a common product structure from which a stream of derivative products can be efficiently developed for different market segments.

**PRODUCTION ORIENTATION**   A make-it-and-sell-it business orientation based on the belief that customers prefer products that are widely available and inexpensive.

**PROMOTION**   As an element of the marketing mix, promotion refers to all the communicative activities used to ensure that customers know about the company's offerings, have a favorable impression of them, and actually make a transaction. These activities include advertising, catalogs, contests, public relations, and personal selling.

**PUBLIC RELATIONS**   A form of communication that aims to increase public awareness and understanding of, and a favorable opinion of, a company, its products, and its services. PR tools include press releases, speeches by executives, and public service activities. Unlike other communication forms, PR operates through unpaid channels.

**RECIPROCAL LINKS**   In Internet marketing, reciprocal links are links with other sites that are generally related to, but not competitive with, the offerings of the host site. For example, a women's clothing site might have a reciprocal link to a women's jewelry site.

**RELATIONSHIP MARKETING**   Building long-term, mutually satisfying relationships with key parties—such as customers, suppliers, and distributors—to earn and retain their long-term business.

**SAMPLE SURVEY**   A market research technique that queries randomized samples of a larger population in a statistically valid way that ensures, within certain limits, that the results can be extrapolated to the larger (unsampled) part of the population.

**SATISFACTION**   A customer's feelings of pleasure or disappointment resulting from comparing a product's perceived performance with the customer's expectations.

**SEGMENTATION**   A market practice that seeks out pieces of the total market that contain customers with identifiable characteristics, as defined by income, age, personal interests, ethnic background, and so forth. The point of segmentation is to focus the marketing effort on a target audience.

**SELLING CONCEPT**   The belief that companies must sell and promote their offerings aggressively because consumers will not buy enough of the offerings on their own.

**SOCIETAL MARKETING CONCEPT**   The belief that a company's task is to identify the needs, wants, and interests of target markets and to deliver the desired satisfactions better than competitors do—but in a way that preserves or enhances consumers' and society's well-being.

**SPAM**   Unrequested and unwanted e-mail.

**STAGE-GATE SYSTEM**   A product or service development system conceived by Robert Cooper that features an alternating series of development stages and assessment "gates" and aims for early elimination of weak ideas and faster time to market for potential winners. These stages and gates control events from the initial idea all the way to commercialization.

**STRATEGY**   A plan that aims to give the enterprise a competitive advantage over rivals. Strategy is about understanding what you do, knowing what you want to become, and—most importantly—focusing on how you plan to get there.

**SUPPLY CHAIN** The long series of activities that results in the creation of raw materials, then components, and then final products that are carried to final buyers. A supply chain includes the marketing channels that bring products to customers.

**TRUE ECONOMIC VALUE (TEV)** A conceptual yardstick for measuring how customers calculate what they are willing to pay:

TEV = Cost of the Best Alternative + Value of Performance Differential

**VALUE** The ratio between what a customer gets and what he or she gives in return.

**VERTICAL PRODUCT LINE** A product line that aims to offer a product for every pocketbook or for different levels of need (e.g., good, better, best).

**WANT** A desire that occurs when a need is directed to specific objects that might satisfy that need; for example, a hamburger is a *want* that might satisfy the *need* for food.

# For Further Reading

## Online Sources

Fresh Focus, www.markitek.com/archives.htm. This biweekly e-newsletter from the consulting firm Markitek is written by founder and market strategist Michael Fischler. Sign up for the online newsletter, and check the site's archive for articles on topics that interest you.

Harvard Business Online, http://harvardbusinessonline.hbsp.harvard.edu. This site provides access to the archive of cases and class notes used at Harvard Business School, as well as to decades of articles published in *Harvard Business Review*. You can search the site for information on marketing, new-product development, pricing, or other topics that interest you. Many of these items can be directly downloaded. All the Harvard sources cited here or in the Notes section can be accessed through this site. (In the spirit of full disclosure, you should know that the site is operated by the publisher of this book.)

Harvard Business School, *Working Knowledge,* http://hbswk.hbs.edu. A free online service of Harvard Business School, *Working Knowledge* provides a steady stream of useful pieces in every business subject area, from business history to technology—and including marketing. These materials take the form of original articles as well as interviews with researchers, practitioners, and authors. The site also includes book reviews and abstracts of the latest research by HBS faculty.

Knowledge@Wharton, http://knowledge.wharton.upenn.edu. This online service of the University of Pennsylvania's Wharton School of Business discusses business trends and provides synopses of research on a variety of topics. Like the HBS site, it can be searched by business topic. You will find many articles on marketing, as well as links to other sources of marketing research.

## Articles

Almquist, Eric, and Gordon Wyner. "Boost Your Marketing ROI with Experimental Design." *Harvard Business Review*, October 2001, 135–141.

Most marketing executives admit that their discipline involves a lot of guesswork. But by borrowing a statistical technique long applied in other fields—experimental design—marketers can develop campaigns that target customers with uncanny accuracy.

Dolan, Robert J. "Analyzing Consumer Preferences." Note 9-599-112 (Boston: Harvard Business School, revised December 12, 2001). Consumer preferences are at the heart of marketing. When we analyze consumer behavior, we typically assess how consumers make purchase decisions. This class note examines two procedures that have proven utility for the actionable analysis of consumer preferences: concept testing and conjoint analysis.

Dolan, Robert J. "Conjoint Analysis: A Manager's Guide." Note 9-590-059 (Boston: Harvard Business School, revised May 8, 1990). This class note describes the technical concept of conjoint analysis in language that managers can understand and follow. It discusses the process by which such a study is done and cites areas of application.

Duta, Ana, James Frary, and Rick Wise. "Finding New Growth in Tough Consumer Markets." *Mercer Management Journal* 17 (Summer 2005): 24–34. Consumer companies face bleak revenue growth prospects due to brand proliferation. This article shows how Kraft, Procter & Gamble, and Netflix are increasing revenue by using their current product positions as starting points to create solutions that reduce the hassles associated with their products.

Hogan, Susan, Eric Almquist, and Simon E. Glynn. "Building a Brand on the Touchpoints That Count." *Mercer Management Journal* 17 (Summer 2005): 46–63. Marketers have many opportunities to "touch" customers with messages. Some are more important than others. This article shows how successful brand builders identify the most critical touch points and invest heavily in them.

Iansiti, Marco, and Alan MacCormack. "Developing Products on Internet Time." *Harvard Business Review* (September–October 1997). The rise of the World Wide Web provided one of the most challenging environments for product development in recent history. The market needs that a product is meant to satisfy and the technologies required to satisfy them can change radically—even as the product is under development. In response to such factors, companies have had to modify the traditional product-development process, in which design implementation begins only after a product's concept has been determined in its entirety. As these authors show, some companies have pioneered a flexible product-development process that allows designers to continue to define and shape products even after implementation has begun. This innovation enables Internet companies to incorporate rapidly evolving customer requirements and changing technologies into their designs until the last possible moment before a product is introduced to the market.

Kon, Martin. "Stop Customer Churn Before It Starts." *Harvard Management Update* (July 2004), 7–8. Satisfaction surveys and exit interviews don't reveal the secret of customer retention. You need to develop a deeper understanding of what really drives customers' behavior. This article offers a three-step approach to understanding the root causes of customer defection.

Rigby, Darrell K., Frederick F. Reichheld, and Phil Schefter. "Avoid the Four Perils of CRM." *Harvard Business Review* (February 2002), 101–109. Measuring and managing loyalty and profitability help you craft an effective customer strategy, something you must articulate, according to these authors, before considering customer relationship management (CRM). Why? CRM technology simply supports your strategy; it doesn't manage customer relationships for you. The authors recommend that you segment customers from the most to the least profitable. Then decide whether to invest in them, to manage the costs of serving them, or to divest them. They also suggest that you avoid stalking customers. Just because CRM allows you to contact them doesn't mean that you always should.

Tabrizi, Behnam, and Rick Walleigh. "Defining Next-Generation Products: An Inside Look." *Harvard Business Review* (November–December 1997). The continued success of technology-based companies depends on their proficiency in creating next-generation products and their derivatives. So getting such products out the door on schedule must be routine for such companies, right? Not quite. Behnam Tabrizi, a consulting professor of engineering management in the Department of Industrial Engineering & Engineering Management at Stanford University, worked with consultant Rick Walleigh on a detailed study of twenty-eight next-generation product-development projects in fourteen leading high-tech companies. The authors had access to sensitive internal information and candid interviews with people at every level. They found that most of the companies were not able to complete such projects on schedule. The companies also had difficulty in developing the derivative products needed to fill the gaps in the market created by their next-generation products. The problem in every case, the authors discovered, was rooted in the product definition phase. And, not coincidentally, all the successful companies in the study had learned how to handle the technical and marketplace uncertainties in their product definition. The authors have discerned from the actions of those companies a set of best practices that can measurably improve the definition phase of any company's product-development process.

Thomke, Stefan, and Ashok Nimgade. "Note on Lead User Research" Note 9-699-014 (Boston: Harvard Business School, 1998). Many of today's greatest products came from the minds of lead users. This 12-page HBS class note describes the lead user concept and presents a step-by-step method for gleaning ideas from this valuable source.

## Books

Aaker, David A. *Building Strong Brands*. New York: Free Press, 1993. Although it's more than twelve years old, this book remains the most authoritative source of ideas on how companies can build brand identity. Aaker uses case studies and reproductions of print ads to show how to align—that is, position—a brand with its target market. The book covers three important issues: (1) why brand managers should avoid myopic focus on brand attributes in favor of emotional and self-expressive factors, (2) the need to understand brands as a "system" that includes overlapping brands and subbrands, and (3) how to use metrics to track brand equity.

Ambler, Tim. *Marketing and the Bottom Line*. 2nd edition. Upper Saddle River, NJ: Prentice Hall, 2004. If you're concerned about the financial value of and ways of measuring marketing investments, this book is well worth reading. One of the greatest errors of marketers is their failure to quantitatively demonstrate that marketing expenditures improve the financial performance of a business. Lacking a connection to the bottom line, is it any wonder that many CEOs are getting stingy about marketing budgets? This book provides clear guidance on how to measure the value of marketing.

Barwise, Patrick, and Seán Meehan. *Simply Better*. Boston: Harvard Business School Press, 2004. Most executives believe that winning and keeping customers require offering something unique. But as products are seen as increasingly hard to differentiate, companies resort to branding, gimmicks, and "thinking outside the box." Meanwhile, customers are less satisfied than they were a decade ago.

Barwise and Meehan argue that most companies have taken differentiation so far that they have left their customers behind. Customers don't want bells and whistles and don't care about trivial differences between brands. What they really want, according to these authors, are quality products, reliable services, and fair value for their money. This book provides an actionable framework for delivering these qualities.

Godin, Seth. *The Big Red Fez: How to Make Any Website Better*. New York: Free Press, 2002. The author of several well-received business books, Seth Godin turns his marketing instincts to the growing field of Web site design. Godin offers practical ideas for making sites more attractive to browsers and buyers. These include avoiding anything that unnecessarily wastes the visitor's time, and giving incentives for clicking through to specific information. Well illustrated throughout.

Humby, Clive, Terry Hunt, and Tim Phillips. *Scoring Points: How Tesco Is Winning Customer Loyalty.* London: Koger Page, 2004. Tesco, a huge U.K. supermarket chain, has also become the world's leading online grocer. But the Tesco site offers more than groceries. It sells CDs, DVDs, books, television sets, insurance products, home mortgages, and even mobile phone services. How did Tesco come this far this fast? The answer lies in its loyalty program and customer database.

As related by two consultants who made it happen, *Scoring Points* tells the story of how Tesco used its "Clubcard" to reinvent itself and create a new relationship with its customers. The book will interest anyone who wants to learn the secrets of loyalty programs, micro-segmentation, and the use of customer data to better understand their needs.

Koehn, Nancy F. *Brand New: How Entrepreneurs Earned Consumers' Trust from Wedgwood to Dell.* Boston: Harvard Business School Press, 2001. Until Josiah Wedgwood, Britons ate from wood or pewter plates. Until Henry Heinz, women toiled to preserve their own pickled foods. Until Michael Dell, few people owned a personal computer, let alone dreamed of buying one built to order. Here, historian Nancy Koehn reveals how these pathfinders shared a powerful gift: the ability to discern how economic and social change would affect consumer needs and wants.

In *Brand New*, Koehn introduces six extraordinary leaders of brand creation—the three just mentioned as well as retailer Marshall Field, cosmetics giant Estée Lauder, and Starbucks founder Howard Schultz. These entrepreneurs, according to Koehn, were more than savvy marketers; they were institution builders who used brands as a vital strategic tool in building powerful capabilities that supported their connections with customers and created new markets.

Kotler, Philip. *Marketing Management.* 11th edition. Upper Saddle River, NJ: Prentice Hall, 2002. Most academics consider this MBA-level textbook the bible of contemporary marketing. Though not intended for working managers, it nevertheless is a handy reference, providing expert coverage of every aspect of modern marketing.

Prahalad, C. K., *Fortune at the Bottom of the Pyramid.* Upper Saddle River, NJ: Prentice Hall, 2004. Although most marketers have their sights on the most affluent segments—people at the top of the income pyramid—C. K. Prahalad contends that the most exciting and rapidly growing market is at the bottom, among the billions of the world's poor. The challenge is to find ways of tapping this huge market profitably. This book shows you how to approach markets in poor countries in ways that can strengthen your bottom line and foster sustainable economic development.

Reichheld, Frederick. *The Loyalty Effect*. Boston: Harvard Business School Press, 2001. The business world seems to have given up on loyalty: many major corporations now lose—and must replace—half their customers in five years, half their employees in four, and half their investors in less than one. Frederick Reichheld shows why companies that ignore these skyrocketing defections face a dismal future of low growth, weak profits, and shortened life expectancy. The author demonstrates the power of loyalty-based management as a highly profitable alternative to the economics of perpetual churn. He makes a powerful economic case for loyalty—and takes readers through the numbers to prove it. His startling conclusion: even a small improvement in customer retention can double profits in your company.

Ries, Al, and Jack Trout. *Marketing Warfare*. New York: McGraw Hill, 1986. This popular and practical book approaches marketing as warfare. The chapter titles tell the tale: "The principle of force," "The superiority of the defense," "Principles of flanking warfare," and so forth. This book is informative and full of ideas. So put on your flak jacket and dive into the trenches.

Wayland, Robert E., and Paul M. Cole. *Customer Connections*. Boston: Harvard Business School Press, 1997. This book provides managers with a strategic framework for making explicit connections between what they know about their customers and how they can leverage that knowledge to create value. Perhaps more than any other book in the field, *Customer Connections* explains how to calculate the financial value of customers, helping readers differentiate between customers who simply consume energy and investment and those who add to company value. Using case examples that include ScrubaDub car wash, *Inc.* magazine, United Parcel Service, and Wachovia Bank, the authors illustrate how exceptional companies have used technology to stay connected to high-value customers.

Wensley, Robin, and Barton A. Weitz, eds. *Handbook of Marketing*. London: Sage Publications, 2002. An excellent complement to our "essentials" book, Wensley and Weitz's *Handbook* covers the field in depth, with individual chapters penned by top people in every field of the marketing discipline. At $130 it's an investment, but one that will pay off if you work regularly in marketing.

Wheelwright, Steven C., and Kim B. Clark. *Revolutionizing Product Development*. New York: Free Press, 1992. Based on years of research and case writing, this book provides a practical architecture for integrating marketing, manufacturing, and design into the important business of product development. That architecture emphasizes the importance of speed, efficiency, and the quality of its output.

# Index

Acela Express, 147–148
aggression factor, 72–73
Almquist, Eric, 90
Amazon.com, 24, 167
Apple, 110
atmospherics, 81

bait and hook pricing, 134–135
Barabba, Vincent, xiv, 33, 44, 118
Barwise, Patrick, 47, 83, 87, 121, 191
Black & Decker, 111–112
Bovet, David, 80
branding
   brand building, 12
   brand defined, 84
   brand equity, 84
   brand extension, 84–85
   brand revitalization, 13–14
   commodity status, 78–79
   differentiation approaches, 81–82
   differentiation of a commodity,
      79–80
   effective differentiation, 86–87
   most recognized brands, 85
   power of, 82–83, 85–86
   product-line extension, 109–112
   summary, 87
breakthrough products, 105–107
buyer preferences analysis
   concept testing, 37–38
   conjoint analysis, 39–41

customer price sensitivity, 41–43
process of, 36

cannibalization issues, 109
CAN–SPAM, 164–165
Cemex, 80
channels, marketing, 25
Cole, Paul, 91
commercialization of a product, 115,
   120
commodity status, 78–79
communications. *See* integrated mar-
      keting communications
competitive strategy, 3–4
competitor analysis
   aggression factor, 72–73
   dynamic market characteristics, 67
   five forces framework, 73–75
   identifying competitors, 67–69
   positioning analysis, 70
   strategies and objectives analysis,
      69–70
   strengths and weaknesses analysis,
      71–72
   summary, 75–76
concept testing, 37–38
conjoint analysis, 39–41
Cooper, Robert, 115
Cordis, 107
Costco, 102
cost–plus pricing, 127–128, 140

customer equity, 92
customer–perceived value, 138–139
customer price sensitivity, 41–43
customer retention
    adjusting to informed consumers,
        186–187
    importance of, 96–97
    learning from defectors, 98–99
    locating the epicenter of defection,
        97–98
    neutralizing causes of defection, 99
    quantifying defection, 97
customer value. See economic value of
    customers
customization. See market
    customization
CVS, 85

Day, George, 66
decline phase of a product, 15
Dell, 24, 72
development, product. See new
    product development
differentiation, product. See branding
direct observation as market research,
    33
distribution, product, 24–26
Dolan, Robert, 41, 138
Drew, Dick, 113–114
Drucker, Peter, xiii
dumping, 179

Earle, Edward Mead, 3
eBay, 3, 11
economic value of customers
    customer development, 99–102
    customer retention, 96–99
    differences in profitability of groups,
        90–92, 201f
    lifetime value calculation, 202f
    range of profitability, 92–94
    steps to improve customer profitabil-
        ity, 94–96
    summary, 102
elasticity of demand, 41–43

e–mail marketing
    best practices, 165–166
    goals, 162
    names and addresses lists, 162–164
    spam, 164–165
empathetic design, 45–47
equity, brand, 84
equity, customer, 92
ethics of marketing, 193–195
Ethics Quality, Inc., 194
experience curve and pricing,
    132–133
experimentation as market research, 33

Fischler, Michael, 192
five forces framework, 73–75
Flint, Peter and Bunny, 80
focus groups as market research, 35
four P's of marketing. See marketing
    mix
future of marketing
    adjusting to informed consumers,
        186–187
    cutting through the clutter, 188–189
    delivering on the promise, 187–188
    ethics of marketing, 193–195
    market fragmentation, 190
    measurement and accountability,
        191–193
    summary, 195

General Motors, xiii, 110, 118
global marketing
    controlling decisions, 180–182
    efficiency versus market suitability,
        175–176
    globalization phenomenon,
        173–174
    market research and, 174–175
    opportunity analysis, 172–173
    place, 178–179
    price, 179–180
    product platform, 176
    promotion, 177–178
    summary, 182–183

"glocal" strategy, 181
Godin, Seth, 188
gray market, 180
growth phase of a product, 11–12

Harley-Davidson, 45–47
horizontal line extensions, 110

IDEO, 46
IMC. *See* integrated marketing
    communications
immersion research, 47–49
incremental products, 106*f*, 107–109
integrated marketing communications
    (IMC)
    challenges for, 153–154
    elements of, 152–153
    goal of, 147–148
    public relations and, 150–151
    summary, 154–155
    vehicle selection, 151–152
    vehicles for, 148–150
interactive marketing. *See* Internet
    marketing
Internet marketing
    adjusting to informed consumers,
        186–187
    benefits for sellers, 160
    e-mail marketing (*see* e-mail
        marketing)
    growing online sales, 158–161
    merchandising, 166–169
    summary, 169
interviews as market research, 35
introduction phase of a product, 10–11

Jordan's Furniture, 81

Koehn, Nancy F., 84
Kotler, Philip, 57, 174, 181

Law of Exclusivity, 62
lead users, 44–45
Lehnerd, Alvin, 110
Leonard, Dorothy, 47

Levitt, Theodore, 173, 174
lifetime value of a customer, 202*f*

Market Basket, 137
market channels, 25
market customization
    downsides to, 62
    mass customization, 53
    microsegments, 60
    positioning the product, 60–62
    segmentation and (*see* segmentation)
    summary, 63
    targeting segments, 58–60
marketing mix
    control of plan implementation,
        28–29
    in global marketing (*see* global
        marketing)
    place, 24–26
    price, 26–27
    product, 22–24
    promotion, 27–28
    summary, 29–30
marketing plan
    elements of, 20–21
    marketing mix (*see* marketing mix)
    purpose of, 20
marketing strategy
    aligning with business strategy, 6–7
    challenges for (*see* future of
        marketing)
    factors impacting, 7–8
    involvement in new product devel-
        opment, 117–118, 120, 121*f*
    market orientation, xiii–xiv
    plan template, 198–200*f*
    process of, 4–5
    product life cycles and (*see* product
        life cycle)
    strategy defined, 2–4
    summary, 16–17
market research
    being outward-looking, 49
    buyer preferences and (*see* buyer
        preferences analysis)

market research, *continued*
  definition and types, 33–35
  empathetic design, 45–47
  global marketing and, 174–175
  immersion, 47–49
  lead users and, 44–45
  people proofing, 44
  positioning the product and, 62
  summary, 50
Martha, Joseph, 80
maturity phase of a product, 12–15
Maytag, 84
Meehan, Seán, 47, 83, 87, 121
Meyer, Marc, 110
microsegments, 60
mission statement, 4
mix, marketing. *See* marketing mix
multifactor segmentation, 55–56

new product development
  breakthrough products, 105–107
  cannibalization issues, 109
  commercialization, 115, 120
  continuous improvement and,
    121–122
  early market exposure for, 118–120
  idea generation, 113–114
  importance of, 104–105
  incremental products, 106f, 107–109
  marketing's involvement in,
    117–118
  market launch, 120
  product-line extension, 109–112
  stage-gate system, 115–116
  strategy development, 120, 121f
  summary, 122–123
Nucor, 79

online selling. *See* Internet marketing
opting in, 163

Packard, David, xiii
Paiva, César, 90
penetration pricing, 130–131, 140

people proofing, 44
Pierce, Andy, 90
Pine, B. Joseph II, 53
place in the marketing mix, 24–26,
    178–179
Porter, Michael, 3, 73, 74, 75
positioning, product, 62
prestige pricing, 133–134
price elasticity of demand, 42–43
price in the marketing mix, 26–27,
    179–180
price skimming strategy, 128–130, 140
pricing strategy
  bait and hook, 134–135
  cost-plus, 127–128, 140
  customer-perceived value, 138–139
  customer price sensitivity, 41–43
  experience curve and, 132–133
  objectives of, 126–127
  penetration pricing, 130–131
  prestige pricing, 133–134
  price skimming, 128–130
  product life cycle and, 139–142
  promotions, 135, 137
  raising prices and, 136
  summary, 142–143
Procter & Gamble, 46, 84
product development. *See* new product
    development
product in the marketing mix, 22–24,
    176
production orientation, xii–xiii
product life cycle
  decline phase, 15
  growth phase, 11–12
  introduction phase, 10–11
  maturity phase, 12–15
  phases overview, 9–10
  pricing strategy and, 139–142
product-line extension, 109–112
product platform, 110–112
promotion in the marketing mix,
    27–28, 177–178
promotions, price, 135, 137

public relations and marketing
    communications, 150–151
purchase data analysis as market
    research, 34
purchase lists, 163–164

Quelch, John, 174

Rayport, Jeffrey, 47
Reichheld, Frederick, 96, 97
research, market. *See* market research
retention, customer. *See* customer
    retention
Ries, Al, 62

Sasser, W. Earl, Jr., 96, 97
segmentation
    of business markets, 57
    multifactor, 55–56
    purpose of, 54–55, 57–58
    relevance and effectiveness of,
        56–57
Shaw's, 137
*Simply Better*, 121
Sloan, Alfred, xiii, 110
Sonnack, Mary, 46

Southwest Airlines, 3, 6, 79
spam and marketing, 164–165
stage-gate system, 115–116
strategy. *See* marketing strategy
Sunbeam, 176
surveys as market research, 34–35
Swatch, 111, 112

targeting segments, 58–60
Tesco, 34
Thomke, Stefan, 46
3M, 46, 113
Trout, Jack, 62
true economic value (TEV), 138

Ulwick, Anthony, 107
USAA, 101

value chain, 100–101
vertical line extensions, 110
von Clausewitz, Carl, 2
von Hippel, Eric, 44, 46

Wayland, Robert, 91

Zaltman, Gerald, 33

# About the Subject Adviser

**PATRICK BARWISE** is Professor of Management and Marketing at London Business School and coauthor (with Seán Meehan, IMD, Lausanne) of *Simply Better: Winning and Keeping Customers by Delivering What Matters Most* (Harvard Business School Press, 2004). Barwise joined LBS in 1976, having spent his early career with IBM. His previous publications include the books *Television and Its Audience, Accounting for Brands, Strategic Decisions, Predictions: Media,* and *Advertising in a Recession,* as well as numerous academic papers and practitioner articles, mostly on brands, consumer and audience behavior, marketing expenditure trends (www.london.edu/marketing/met), and new media. Barwise is also an adviser to the U.K. communications regulator Ofcom, and he recently led an independent review for the U.K. government of the BBC's digital television services.

# About the Writer

**RICHARD LUECKE** is the writer of many books in the Harvard Business Essentials series. Based in Salem, Massachusetts, Mr. Luecke has authored or developed more than forty books and dozens of articles on a wide range of business subjects. He has an M.B.A. from the University of St. Thomas. He can be reached at richard.luecke@verizon.net.

| Title | Product # |
|---|---|
| Harvard Business Review on **Decision Making** | 5572 |
| Harvard Business Review on **Developing Leaders** | 5003 |
| Harvard Business Review on **Doing Business in China** | 6387 |
| Harvard Business Review on **Effective Communication** | 1437 |
| Harvard Business Review on **Entrepreneurship** | 9105 |
| Harvard Business Review on **Finding and Keeping the Best People** | 5564 |
| Harvard Business Review on **Innovation** | 6145 |
| Harvard Business Review on **The Innovative Enterprise** | 130X |
| Harvard Business Review on **Knowledge Management** | 8818 |
| Harvard Business Review on **Leadership** | 8834 |
| Harvard Business Review on **Leadership at the Top** | 2756 |
| Harvard Business Review on **Leadership in a Changed World** | 5011 |
| Harvard Business Review on **Leading in Turbulent Times** | 1806 |
| Harvard Business Review on **Managing Diversity** | 7001 |
| Harvard Business Review on **Managing High-Tech Industries** | 1828 |
| Harvard Business Review on **Managing People** | 9075 |
| Harvard Business Review on **Managing Projects** | 6395 |
| Harvard Business Review on **Managing the Value Chain** | 2344 |
| Harvard Business Review on **Managing Uncertainty** | 9083 |
| Harvard Business Review on **Managing Your Career** | 1318 |
| Harvard Business Review on **Marketing** | 8040 |
| Harvard Business Review on **Measuring Corporate Performance** | 8826 |
| Harvard Business Review on **Mergers and Acquisitions** | 5556 |
| Harvard Business Review on **Mind of the Leader** | 6409 |
| Harvard Business Review on **Motivating People** | 1326 |
| Harvard Business Review on **Negotiation** | 2360 |
| Harvard Business Review on **Nonprofits** | 9091 |
| Harvard Business Review on **Organizational Learning** | 6153 |
| Harvard Business Review on **Strategic Alliances** | 1334 |
| Harvard Business Review on **Strategies for Growth** | 8850 |
| Harvard Business Review on **Teams That Succeed** | 502X |
| Harvard Business Review on **Turnarounds** | 6366 |
| Harvard Business Review on **What Makes a Leader** | 6374 |
| Harvard Business Review on **Work and Life Balance** | 3286 |

# Harvard Business Essentials

In the fast-paced world of business today, everyone needs a personal re-source—a place to go for advice, coaching, background information, or an-swers. The Harvard Business Essentials series fits the bill. Concise and straightforward, these books provide highly practical advice for readers at all levels of experience. Whether you are a new manager interested in ex-panding your skills or an experienced executive looking to stay on top, these solution-oriented books give you the reliable tips and tools you need to im-prove your performance and get the job done. Harvard Business Essentials titles will quickly become your constant companions and trusted guides.

**These books are priced at $19.95 U.S., except as noted.**
**Price subject to change.**

| Title | Product # |
|---|---|
| Harvard Business Essentials: **Negotiation** | 1113 |
| Harvard Business Essentials: **Managing Creativity and Innovation** | 1121 |
| Harvard Business Essentials: **Managing Change and Transition** | 8741 |
| Harvard Business Essentials: **Hiring and Keeping the Best People** | 875X |
| Harvard Business Essentials: **Finance for Managers** | 8768 |
| Harvard Business Essentials: **Business Communication** | 113X |
| Harvard Business Essentials: **Manager's Toolkit ($24.95)** | 2896 |
| Harvard Business Essentials: **Managing Projects Large and Small** | 3213 |
| Harvard Business Essentials: **Creating Teams with an Edge** | 290X |
| Harvard Business Essentials: **Entrepreneur's Toolkit** | 4368 |
| Harvard Business Essentials: **Coaching and Mentoring** | 435X |
| Harvard Business Essentials: **Crisis Management** | 4376 |
| Harvard Business Essentials: **Time Management** | 6336 |
| Harvard Business Essentials: **Power, Influence, and Persuasion** | 631X |
| Harvard Business Essentials: **Strategy** | 6328 |
| Harvard Business Essentials: **Decision Making** | 7618 |

# The Results-Driven Manager

The Results-Driven Manager series collects timely articles from Harvard Management Update and Harvard Management Communication Letter to help senior to middle managers sharpen their skills, increase their effectiveness, and gain a competitive edge. Presented in a concise, accessible format to save managers valuable time, these books offer authoritative insights and techniques for improving job performance and achieving immediate results.

**These books are priced at $14.95 U.S.**
**Price subject to change.**

| Title | Product # |
|---|---|
| The Results-Driven Manager: | |
| **Face-to-Face Communications for Clarity and Impact** | 3477 |
| The Results-Driven Manager: | |
| **Managing Yourself for the Career You Want** | 3469 |
| The Results-Driven Manager: | |
| **Presentations That Persuade and Motivate** | 3493 |
| The Results-Driven Manager: **Teams That Click** | 3507 |
| The Results-Driven Manager: | |
| **Winning Negotiations That Preserve Relationships** | 3485 |
| The Results-Driven Manager: **Dealing with Difficult People** | 6344 |
| The Results-Driven Manager: **Taking Control of Your Time** | 6352 |
| The Results-Driven Manager: **Getting People on Board** | 6360 |
| The Results-Driven Manager: | |
| **Motivating People for Improved Performance** | 7790 |
| The Results-Driven Manager: **Becoming an Effective Leader** | 7804 |
| The Results-Driven Manager: | |
| **Managing Change to Reduce Resistance** | 7812 |
| The Results-Driven Manager: | |
| **Hiring Smart for Competitive Advantage** | 9726 |
| The Results-Driven Manager: **Retaining Your Best People** | 9734 |
| The Results-Driven Manager: | |
| **Business Etiquette for the New Workplace** | 9742 |

## How to Order

Harvard Business School Press publications are available worldwide from your local bookseller or online retailer.
You can also call

### 1-800-668-6780

Our product consultants are available to help you
8:00 a.m.–6:00 p.m., Monday–Friday, Eastern Time.
Outside the U.S. and Canada, call: 617-783-7450
Please call about special discounts for quantities greater than ten.

You can order online at

### www.HBSPress.org